"Alone on the Wall is a testament to the spectacular accomplishments that come with tremendous drive and self-control. Typically humble and understated, Honnold recounts in his own words the seven most astonishing achievements thus far in his meteoric career."
—*360 Magazine*

"Alone on the Wall is a fast-paced, vertigo-inducing, gloriously wild read chock-full of amped-up adventures and occasional misadventures across the globe."
—Bookreporter.com

"Remarkable commentary providing an intense, white-knuckle reading experience. . . . [B]reathtaking."
—*Mazama Bulletin*

"It's sure to get the palms sweating."
—*DPM Climbing*

Praise for
ALEX **HONNOLD**

"The closest thing to a celebrity that American rock climbing offers."
—*New York Times*

"[Honnold] is best known for his fearless ascents of the world's biggest cliffs. . . . He has traversed them all with his bare hands, fingertips jammed into crevices and clinging to half-inch shelves of protruding rock to hold his chiseled 5' 11", 160-pound frame."
—*Sports Illustrated*

"Honnold climbs longer and more difficult routes than anyone previously thought possible. . . . He also climbs them in record time."
—*Atlantic*

"Alex Honnold has become arguably the most well-known and widely respected climber in the world." —*Interview*

"Honnold is the biggest name in a group of adventure athletes engaging in high-risk live action-sports spectacles that seem to be pulled from the Evel Knievel playbook." —*Outside*

"He's utterly genuine. There's no bullshit there." —Jon Krakauer, mountaineer and *New York Times* best-selling author

"When you meet Alex Honnold, you're gonna be like, 'Huh, this guy is a bumbling, dorky, awkward goofball.' Until he steps on the rock, and then he's literally a whole other person. He becomes this poised, graceful, calculated badass dude." —Cedar Wright, Honnold's regular climbing partner

"Honnold's on another level than anyone else out there. It's like he doesn't feel fear or any of the normal emotions that anyone else feels. He has this ability to just shut his brain off and do the sickest climbs that have ever been done." —Nick Martino, climber

ALONE ON THE WALL

Alex Honnold
with David Roberts

W. W. NORTON & COMPANY
INDEPENDENT PUBLISHERS SINCE 1923
NEW YORK   LONDON

*To my family, for always supporting me
along an unconventional path*

For information about permission to reproduce selections from this book,
write to Permissions, W. W. Norton & Company, Inc.,
500 Fifth Avenue, New York, NY 10110

For information about special discounts for bulk purchases, please contact
W. W. Norton Special Sales at specialsales@wwnorton.com or 800-233-4830

Manufacturing by Quad Graphics Fairfield
Book design by Lovedog Studio
Production manager: Julia Druskin

Library of Congress Cataloging-in-Publication Data

Names: Honnold, Alex.
Title: Alone on the wall / Alex Honnold with David Roberts.
Description: First Edition. | New York : W.W. Norton & Company, [2016] | Includes index.
Identifiers: LCCN 2015027977 | ISBN 9780393247626 (hardcover)
Subjects: LCSH: Honnold, Alex. | Mountaineers—United States—Biography.
Classification: LCC GV199.92.H67 A3 2016 | DDC 796.522092—dc23
LC record available at http://lccn.loc.gov/2015027977

ISBN 978-0-393-35317-4 pbk.

W. W. Norton & Company, Inc.
500 Fifth Avenue, New York, N.Y. 10110
www.wwnorton.com

W. W. Norton & Company Ltd.
15 Carlisle Street, London W1D 3BS

1 2 3 4 5 6 7 8 9 0

Contents

CHAPTER **ONE**
MOONLIGHT

I started up the climb shortly after dawn. I wasn't even sure I'd found the right start, since I hadn't been on these lower pitches for two or three years. The beginning of the route is kind of scruffy and ambiguous—ramps, traverses, and hand cracks angling up to the right—but it's not as difficult as the upper two-thirds of the wall.

Still, I was nervous, even a little giddy. It had rained pretty much nonstop the day before, and now the rock was sandy, slabby, and a lot damper than I'd hoped. I probably should have waited another day before heading up the route. But I was overpsyched. I couldn't bear the thought of sitting in my van another whole day, thinking the same thoughts I had recycled for the past forty-eight hours. I had to strike while the iron was hot.

Moonlight Buttress is a 1,200-foot-high, nearly vertical sandstone cliff in Utah's Zion National Park. It may be the finest—the purest and most classic—route among Zion's thousands of lines. It's also one of the most continuously difficult crack climbs in the world.

The first ascent of Moonlight Buttress came in October 1971, when Jeff Lowe and Mike Weis, two legends of American climbing, pioneered the route. It took them a day and a half, with an overnight bivouac on a ledge in the middle of the wall. They used a lot of aid, pulling or hanging on expansion bolts and pitons.

Nearly twenty-one years later, in April 1992, Peter Croft and Johnny Woodward made the first free ascent, as they took all the aid out of the route by finding sequences of moves they could climb without hanging on gear. They solved the route in nine pitches (rope lengths), but rated the climb a really stiff 5.13a (since downgraded to 5.12d). In 1992, that was near the upper limit of free-climbing difficulty anywhere in the world, and Croft and Woodward's feat was a brilliant one.

Peter Croft was already one of my heroes, because in the 1980s and '90s he had pushed free soloing—climbing without a rope or gear at all—to unprecedented extremes. Many of the routes he'd free soloed back then had never been repeated in that style during the decades since.

But as far as I knew, no one had even thought of free soloing Moonlight Buttress. That's what I was hoping to pull off on April 1, 2008.

In the back of my mind was a nagging worry about the feature called the Rocker Blocker. It's an ample ledge, about half the size of a queen-size bed, at the top of the third pitch. Because it's loose, somebody has chained it in place with a two-bolt anchor, but it actually makes for a good stance about 400 feet off the ground.

It wasn't the ledge itself that fueled my angst. From the Rocker Blocker, stretching on tiptoe, you can just reach a key hold above. Essentially you face a 5.12c boulder problem right off the ledge. You don't actually have to jump to make the move, but it's more like an upward lurch to a small edge. As I climbed the easy pitches down low, that move loomed over me. I was pretty sure I could stick the ledge if I fell off, but I'd sure hate to find out.

The day before, sitting in my van in the rain, I had deliberately visualized everything that might happen on the climb. Including breaking a hold, or just losing it and falling off. I saw myself bouncing off the ledge below and going all the way to the ground, fracturing most of my bones as I rag-dolled down the mountain. I'd probably bleed out at the base.

I hadn't slept very well the previous night. So I got the early start in the morning that I'd planned, hoping to beat the sun to the wall and get cool conditions on the route. To reach the base of Moonlight Buttress, you have to wade the Virgin River, which in early April was freezing-ass cold. I forded the stream barefoot. The rushing water came up above my knees. My feet quickly went numb, and my whole body went into mild shock. Plus I had to pay attention to my balance as I placed my feet carefully in the gaps between polished river cobbles.

At what I thought was the start of Moonlight Buttress, I cached my approach shoes and my daypack. I'd decided to carry nothing— neither food, nor water, nor spare clothes—up the route. I clipped on my chalk bag and laced up my rock shoes. My feet were still cold, but they weren't truly numb—I could feel my toes all right. I was wearing only shorts and a T-shirt. At the last minute, I put on headphones and turned up my iPod. I was shuffling through my own Top 25 playlist of tunes—mostly punk and modern rock.

It may sound lame, but I didn't have a watch, and I was pretty sure I was going to set the speed record for Moonlight Buttress. I could use the iPod to measure the exact number of minutes the climb would take. Music also has a way of helping you focus, although nowadays I prefer to climb without my iPod, because I consider it a bit of a crutch.

· · · ·

For me, free soloing a big wall is all about preparation. In a real sense, I had performed the hard work on Moonlight Buttress during the days leading up to the climb. Once I was on the route, it was just a matter of executing.

Yes, I'd climbed the whole route only once before, with a philosophy professor named Bill Ramsey. In his midforties, he was still climbing really well, and he'd been working on freeing Moonlight. He recruited me to climb it with him for his free attempt, and we swung leads up the whole route. It was a great day as we both climbed the route clean with no falls.

But that was two or three years earlier. In the days before my free solo attempt, I'd focused on the upper 800 feet of the route. It's a mellow hike along a paved trail to the top of Moonlight Buttress, so I hauled up 600 feet of rope, rappelled down it, and practiced the moves on toprope. To self-belay, I used a device called a Mini Traxion, which grips the rope on a downward pull but slides effortlessly up the rope as you climb. If I fell or even rested, the Mini Traxion would hold me tight.

With my toprope, I climbed the upper 600 feet of Moonlight Buttress twice. The crux of the whole route—the hardest single passage, which is the make-or-break stretch of an ascent—is an amazing clean inside corner, 180 feet long. It's the fourth of nine pitches on the route, and it's what gives the climb its 5.12d rating. It's continuous and really strenuous, so your arms get pretty pumped by the time you reach the top of it.

Each toproped rehearsal of those upper 600 feet had taken me only about an hour. I felt super-solid. At no point did I fall off or even feel sketchy. But then I realized that the 600-foot rope didn't reach down to a crucial 5.11c rightward traverse on the third pitch. So the next day I went back up to the top with 800 feet of rope, rapped down again, and rehearsed the traverse moves until I had them dialed too.

I ran into a few other climbers on my practice runs. I even rescued an aid-climbing chick who didn't quite know what she was doing and had gotten stuck on her lead. I yelled, "Hey, grab this rope!" as I swung the tail of my fixed rope to her, so she could liberate herself from her trap. She was pretty grateful. It's not every day that somebody comes rapping out of the sky on a route like that.

Then came two days of rain. I sat in my van in a movie theater parking lot in Springdale, stared out the windshield, and thought.

I'd gone to a movie to pass the time, but the rest of the day, into the evening, and through most of the second day I sat in the van, just thinking. It's not like I had work to do. I didn't have anything to do except think. About the climb.

Sitting and thinking, hour after hour. Visualizing every single move, everything that could possibly happen. That's what it takes to wrap your mind around a challenge such as the one I was about to attempt.

That's what I mean by preparation. Now I'd find out if I'd prepared adequately—if I could simply execute what I'd visualized, every handhold and foothold on the long way to the top of the wall.

A T THE END OF MARCH 2008, Alex Honnold was little known beyond the small circle of his friends. Seven years later, at the age of thirty, he is probably the most famous climber in the world. That's not to claim that he's the best climber in the world—in fact, there's no such thing as the "best climber," because the sport has subdivided into so many genres, from Himalayan mountaineering to bouldering in indoor gyms.

The reason for Honnold's meteoric celebrity is that he's pushed the most extreme and dangerous form of climbing far beyond the limits of what anyone thought was possible. Free soloing means climbing without a rope, a partner, or any "hardware" (pitons, nuts, or cams) to attach oneself to the wall. In its stark simplicity, that pursuit can be understood by the most casual observer. The stakes are ultimate: *If you fall, you die.*

What Alex has done is to free solo routes both longer and of much greater difficulty than anyone before him has thought possible. So far, he's gotten away with it, though some of his closest friends are afraid that he's going to kill himself.

Free soloing is far more than a stunt. It amounts to reducing climbing to its most elemental challenge: a man (or woman), with only rock shoes on his feet and chalk on his fingertips for better purchase, against the cliff. It's climbing at its absolute purest.

This is not the only kind of climbing Alex does, however. His speed "linkups"—enchainments of two or three big wall climbs back-to-back against the stopwatch, with only a minimal reliance on ropes or protection—have rewritten the book in Yosemite. And since 2013, Alex has expanded his horizons to mountaineering, where he's already doing things no one else has managed to pull off.

Alex Honnold, in short, is a climbing visionary, of the sort who comes along maybe once in a generation. He's also smart, funny, a man with surprisingly little ego, and a person who wants to make the world a better place for people less privileged or talented than he is. Nearly everyone who knows or even just watches Alex likes him, because, as Jon Krakauer says, "He's utterly genuine. There's no bullshit there."

Again and again, whenever he speaks in public, Alex is asked the same two questions by everyone from little kids to graybeards. Indeed, they are the fundamental questions about what he's doing on rock. They are:

Aren't you afraid you're going to die?
Why do you do this?

In a sense, those questions are unanswerable. They lie in the realm of George Leigh Mallory's throwaway response in 1923 to the umpteenth journalist who asked him why he wanted to climb Everest: "Because it is there." (Though intended as an irritable jab by a man fed up with the question, Mallory's quip has become the most famous quotation in mountaineering history.)

Alex has come up with his own quips to answer the inevitable questions. About falling to his death: "It'll be the worst four seconds of my life." And: "I'm sure half the people will say, 'At least he died doing what he loved best.' And the other half will say, 'What a fucking douche!'"

Alex is unmistakably a driven, competitive fellow. Yet his modesty, born of an innate shyness, takes the form of radical understatement of his accomplishments, verging (like the quips above) on self-deprecation. His nickname among his closest climbing buddies is Alex "No Big Deal" Honnold.

In the last forty years, only a handful of climbers have pushed free soloing to the razor edge of risk. Half of them are dead. Some of those soloists have survived their decades of dancing above the abyss: they include not only Peter Croft but also Henry Barber, who crisscrossed the globe in the 1970s, blowing the minds of locals at crags from Wales to Australia by flashing their hardest routes.

Others died when a single mistake caught up to them. Among their number was Derek Hersey, a Brit transplanted to the States, who fell to his death in 1993 on the Steck-Salathé route in Yosemite, possibly because a rainstorm slickened the holds. Dan Osman, Charlie Fowler, and Michael Reardon also died in accidents related to their pursuit of extreme exploits on cliffs and mountains. But the demise that most shocked the climbing world was that of John Bachar, with Peter Croft one of the two outstanding soloists of the 1980s and '90s. After thirty-five years of climbing route after route without a rope, Bachar fell off a short climb he had done many times before, on a route near his home in Mammoth Lakes, California, in July 2009.

Alex points out that none of this group of elite climbers died while pushing their limits at free soloing. Hersey and Bachar fell off routes that would normally have been well within their capacities. (There was speculation that a spinal problem that caused his left arm and shoulder suddenly to weaken, the result of a recent car accident, might have caused Bachar's fatal fall.) Reardon was swept to his death by a rogue wave after he had soloed *down* to the base of a sea cliff in Ireland. Fowler died in an avalanche as he attempted an unclimbed mountain in western China. Osman met his end while pushing to new extremes a sport he had virtually invented— rope jumping, or deliberately leaping off a cliff to be caught by the rope or ropes he was tied into. Having set a record jump of more than a thousand feet, Osman died when his rope broke on a plunge off Leaning Tower in Yosemite.

Still, all five of those extreme free soloists were out there on the cutting edge of adventure when they perished. Osman in effect discovered the boundaries of rope jumping by paying for the experiment with his life. Though still alive and well at sixty-two, Henry Barber came perilously close to falling to his death in the early 1980s as he was filmed free soloing a British sea-cliff route for an American TV show. Distracted by a nearby cameraman's sudden movement, Barber lost his balance. As he later described that moment,

> It caught me the wrong way. . . . I was doing some stemming moves, pushing with both hands against the sides of the groove. I pushed just a little too hard and my left shoulder bumped the wall, so that I started to fall. Adrenaline shot from my toes right up to my head. . . . I was off and headed down. But the balance and flow of all the movement that had gone on until that point carried me through, keeping me on the rock and still moving.

With his sharp intelligence, Alex inclines toward a hyperrational take on life. He actually insists, "I don't like risk. I don't like passing over double yellow. I don't like rolling the dice." He distinguishes between consequences and risk. Obviously, the consequences of a fall while free soloing are ultimate ones. But that doesn't mean, he argues, that he's taking ultimate risks. As he puts it, "I always call risk the likelihood of actually falling off. The consequence is what will happen if you do. So I try to keep my soloing low-risk—as in, I'm not likely to fall off, even though there'd be really high consequences if I did."

Just as rational, on the other hand, are some of the arguments made by close friends of Alex who worry about the chances he's taking. Seven years Alex's senior, Tommy Caldwell has been his partner on marathon linkups and mountaineering expeditions. One of the best rock climbers in the world, as well as one of the role models Alex most admires, Caldwell said in 2011, "I've never tried to free solo anything really grand. I've fallen completely unexpectedly lots of times—maybe a dozen—on relatively easy terrain, when a hold broke off or the rubber peeled off the sole of my shoe, or something. If I'd been soloing, I'd have died.

"I really like Alex. I don't want him to die."

•   •   •   •

By now, the audience Alex commands stretches far beyond the ranks of hardcore climbers. He's known, for instance, as "that kid Lara Logan interviewed on *60 Minutes*," or as "the guy in that amazing photo on the cover of *National Geographic*." But for nonclimbers fully to understand exactly what Alex is doing, a brief primer in techniques, gear, and grade ratings is necessary.

In conventional rock climbing, a pair of climbers is connected with a nylon rope usually about sixty meters (almost 200 feet) in length. One climber, anchored safely to the wall, belays the leader as he climbs above. To minimize the consequences of a fall, the leader places protection ("pro") as he goes.

Throughout most of the history of rock climbing, the leader would hammer a piton—any of an assortment of differently shaped metal spikes, first made of iron but now improved with chrome-molybdenum steel alloy—into a natural crack in the rock surface. Once the piton was firmly driven, the leader clipped a carabiner—an oval link with a spring-loaded gate—into the eye of the piton, then fed the rope through the 'biner. That way, if he fell, say, five feet above the piton, the belayer on the other end of the rope could stop his fall after a plunge of only a little more than ten feet—the additional footage due to the stretchiness of the nylon rope, which also cushions the jolt.

By the 1980s, pitons had become passé except in big-range mountaineering, because the repeated hammering as they were driven home and then pried loose damaged the rock, leaving ugly "pin scars." Instead, climbers started using nuts—variously shaped blobs of metal that could be slotted into cracks and wrinkles in the rock so they'd hold tight under a downward pull. Nuts, in general, are much less secure than pitons. In the late 1970s, Ray Jardine invented ingenious devices he called "Friends" (now more generically referred to as "cams"). They're spring-loaded gizmos with opposing semicircular plates. You pull a kind of trigger that retracts the plates, slot the cam into a crack that wouldn't hold a nut, then release the trigger. The spring allows the plates to grip the edges of the crack, and a well-placed cam can hold weights of thousands of pounds. Needless to say, cams have revolutionized rock climbing.

From the earliest days onward, climbers surmounted otherwise unclimbable stretches of rock by using their pro as artificial holds. This is called "direct aid," or simply "aid." Whole pitches of aid can be negotiated with *étriers* or aiders—nylon slings with three or four foot loops to make flexible ladders. The aid climber hangs an aider from a piton or nut or cam, then climbs the nylon rungs rather than the rock itself.

Eventually, expansion bolts enlarged the technical arsenal. In blank rock devoid of cracks, the climber bores a hollow sleeve, either by hammer or mechanical drill. Into that sleeve he then hammers the cylindrical bolt, usually made of stainless steel. A hanger, similar to the eye of a piton, is affixed to the head of the bolt. Then the climber attaches a carabiner to the hanger and clips in his rope. A good bolt is as strong as the best piton.

Free climbing, as opposed to free soloing, means that the leader uses his protection only to safeguard a fall. He does not slot a nut or cam and then pull on it to move upward. He climbs the rock with only his hands and feet, but if he falls on solid pro, he's not likely to be injured.

In the United States, rock routes climbed free are rated on a scale of difficulty, called the Yosemite Decimal System (YDS), that currently ranges from 5.1 to 5.15. The reason for the awkward numbering is that in the US experts long believed that no climbs harder than 5.9 would ever be accomplished. By the late 1960s, however, that limit had been transcended, and the classifiers felt they had no choice but to invent 5.10. The system is inherently conservative, so the higher grades, such as 5.13, have been subdivided into four classes of their own, ranging from 5.13a through 5.13d. Top-notch climbers recognize that there is as great a gap in difficulty between 5.13b and 5.13c as between 5.8 and 5.9.

At the moment, the hardest climbs in the world, of which there are only a handful, are rated 5.15c.

In the last twenty years, expansion bolts have given rise to the phenomenon of "sport" climbing—as distinguished from "trad" (short for "traditional"), in which climbers place and remove nuts and cams for protection. On a sport route, permanent bolts placed as closely as six or eight feet apart, often driven on rappel before the route has been attempted, allow climbers to get up very hard free routes on rock that won't take cams or nuts, with almost bomb-proof safety. The leader simply clips into one bolt after another as he climbs. For the belayer, catching the leader's fall is routine.

Sport climbing has skyrocketed in popularity in recent years. There are now hotshot teenagers who can climb 5.14 sport routes but who have never led a single pitch of trad, and wouldn't have a clue how to do so.

Because the YDS 5.1 to 5.15 system measures only the pure difficulty of the hardest move, nearly all the top-rated climbs in the world are on short sport routes on easily accessible crags. To put up a 5.15 route, an expert such as Chris Sharma or Adam Ondra will "work" the sequence of moves for weeks or even months on end, falling harmlessly hundreds of times, before he can complete the climb in one try without a single fall. That kind of climbing is so specialized that the Ondras of the world practice almost no other art.

Ironically, then, trad climbing is more "sporting" than sport climbing—and more daring and dangerous.

But free soloing is another whole game. When Alex Honnold performs one of his long free solos, he does away altogether with ropes, with a partner to catch his fall, with pro of any kind (no bolts, pitons, nuts, or cams) to use for artificial holds or to safeguard a fall. Because the chances of falling on even a 5.11 or 5.12 climb are considerable, only a few practitioners have dared to push free soloing beyond the 5.11 level—and then usually on short routes, and only after "rehearsing" the line by climbing it with a rope and a partner many times to memorize every hold and sequence. (For that matter, when you're climbing without a rope, you can fall off and die on a 5.4 route if a handhold or foothold breaks loose.)

Free soloing, then, is the most sporting—the purest—form of rock climbing ever devised. It's the ultimate adventure on rock—with the ultimate stakes if you make the slightest mistake.

People ask me all the time how I got into free soloing. But I don't think they quite believe me when I give an honest answer. The truth is that when I started climbing outdoors, I was too shy to go up to strangers at a crag and ask if they'd like to rope up with me.

I first started climbing at age ten at an indoor gym in my home-town of Sacramento, California, but I did very little outdoors before the age of nineteen. I was so antisocial and tweaky that I was actually afraid to talk to strangers. Though I was already climbing 5.13, I would never have gotten up the nerve to approach other guys at a crag like Lover's Leap near Lake Tahoe and ask if I could rope up with them.

So I just started soloing. The first route I did was a low-angle 5.5 slab called Knapsack Crack at Lover's Leap. Then I tackled a much steeper three-pitch route called Corrugation Corner, rated 5.7. I overgripped the shit out of it, because I was really scared and climbing badly.

But I quickly got better. I've always been a compulsive ticker. From the very start, I kept a bound notebook in which I recorded every climb I did, each one with a brief note. My "climbing bible," as I called it, was my most precious possession. In 2005 and 2006, I did tons of routes at Joshua Tree, on the granite boulders and pinnacles in the desert east of Los Angeles. I developed a voracious appetite for soloing. I'd do as many as fifty pitches in a day, mostly on short routes up to 5.10. A sample entry from my bible:

10/7/05

18 pitches—kind of a low-day

5.7 to [5].10b

I couldn't start the left Peyote Crack. Weird.

I soon got so that I felt pretty comfortable soloing. I discovered that if I had any particular gift, it was a mental one—the ability to keep it together in what might otherwise have been a stressful situation. By 2007, I had soloed a few pitches up to 5.12a in difficulty. I felt like I was ready for a big next step.

Still, back then I had no thought of becoming a professional climber, or even of attracting any attention for what I did. In September 2007, I went to Yosemite. I had my eye on two legendary routes—the north face of the Rostrum, a beautiful 800-foot granite pillar, rated 5.11c, and Astroman on Washington Column, a touchstone 1,100-foot route, also rated 5.11c.

Way back in 1987, Peter Croft had stunned the climbing world by free soloing both routes in a single day. No one had repeated that feat in twenty years. Of the two climbs, Astroman is significantly harder and more serious—more physically taxing and more insecure. Only one other guy had free soloed Astroman—Dean Potter in 2000. Still climbing hard at age forty-three, Potter has recently specialized in combining hard routes with wingsuit BASE jumping. He was another influential free soloist I looked up to as a role model.

On September 19, I free soloed both Astroman and the Rostrum. I'd climbed both routes before roped up with partners, but I couldn't say that I had either route dialed. I was glad that day to find no one else on either climb. I didn't tell anybody beforehand what I was going to try. I just showed up and did them. They went really well—I felt in control the whole way on both climbs. In my "bible," I noted only

9/19/07

Astroman—5.11c—solo

Rostrum—5.11c—" "

I added a smiley face after Astroman, but no other comments.

That evening I called a friend (it might have been Chris Weidner) and told him about my day. That's how the word got out. I'll admit that the double solo stirred up a certain buzz in the Valley (as climbers call Yosemite), but only among the hardcore locals. In my mind, the fact that I did both routes in one day, just as Peter Croft had, wasn't particularly significant. What was significant was committing to doing them at all. And succeeding gave me the confidence to start imagining even bigger free solos.

• • • •

Five months later, in February 2008, I drove to Indian Creek in southern Utah. The Creek is a mecca of short, beautiful cracks on solid Wingate sandstone. I was in terrific form there, climbing roped up with various partners. I onsighted the hardest routes, getting up them on my first try without falling. Routes up to 5.13b or c. But I'd been climbing so much, I'd developed a bad case of tendinitis in my left elbow. At first I didn't even know what was wrong—I thought I'd hurt my biceps from sheer overuse. But at the Creek, after only two or three pitches, the pain was so intense I'd have to shut it down. One day on, then two days off. I'd go mountain biking with my friend Cedar Wright, just trying to mix it up. But it drove me crazy not to be able to climb more.

Weirdly enough, by contributing to my general angst, the tendinitis was good for Moonlight Buttress. It takes a certain hunger to be motivated to go do something big. At the Creek, I was so fit and climbing so well, but I was also hungry to do more, because I had to limit my days on rock to a lot fewer than I wanted.

And Moonlight Buttress was a project I'd been dreaming of for years, ever since Bill Ramsey and I had climbed it a few years before. Which is why I found myself in Zion, sitting in my van all day in the rain on March 30 and 31, 2008, visualizing everything that could possibly happen on that amazing route the next day.

All the soloing I had done during the previous several years had taught me the value of preparation. But I'd never prepared for a free solo as diligently as I did for Moonlight. Rehearsing the moves on toprope for two days until I had every sequence lodged in my memory was crucial, but so were those days of just sitting and thinking. Imagining every placement of each hand and foot all the way up the huge route. Visualizing everything that could happen. . . . In a real sense, I performed the hard work of that free solo during the days leading up to it. Once I was on the climb, it was just a matter of executing.

The dampness and sandiness of the lower part of the wall had addled me somewhat. And at first, I was confused as to whether I was actually on-route. I wasn't truly scared—just hesitant and uncertain. In retrospect, I think I projected my anxiety about the whole project, as I'd sat in my van visualizing it for two days, onto the start of the climb. Now I was driven upward by pure excitement, which always has an edge of anxiety about it.

The second pitch is a clean splitter crack, and once I got onto that, I knew I was on-route. There's really only one line to the summit. And after that second pitch, the rock dried out and the sandiness pretty much disappeared. As I climbed higher, I steadily gained confidence. The 5.11c rightward traverse on the third pitch went like clockwork. By the time I got to the Rocker Blocker ledge, it was "Game on!" I was making the moves with what felt like perfect execution.

As I started off the Rocker Blocker toward the tricky boulder problem, the scenario of coming off and trying to stick the ledge was in the back of my mind. But I was moving efficiently, and as soon as I made the little upward lurch and seized the crucial handhold, I knew I wouldn't come off. My confidence surged even higher.

Above the Rocker Blocker, I started up the 180-foot 5.12d

inside corner that's the crux of the whole route. That stern rating doesn't derive from any single particularly hard move, but from the strenuous continuity of the whole thing. And here's where my preparation paid off. I started up the corner stemming—placing the edges of my feet carefully on tiny wrinkles of sandstone on either side of the central crack, then moving smoothly upward from one hold to the next. The wall here is dead vertical, so you have to gauge those holds precisely. But I remembered every one from my toprope rehearsal. Also, as I had expected, the wall here, which is protected from the rain by a small roof far above, was totally dry.

I was able to rest here and there on small holds as I stemmed up the first eighty feet of the corner. But then I had to shift from stemming to liebacking. Now I grabbed the edge of the crack with both hands, leaned back to the left, and walked my feet up the opposite wall till the soles of my shoes were only two feet below my lower hand. Liebacking feels somewhat unnatural. The whole key to moving upward is the stability provided by the pull with your hands counterbalancing the push with your feet. The position you're in is almost like sitting in a rowing shell and pulling hard on the oars. You methodically alternate feet and hand movements as you inch up the crack. Yes, it's strenuous, but a clean lieback feels solid and secure. If the edges of the crack aren't sharp or are flared outward, though, or the wall you place your feet on is too slick, liebacking is pretty scary. You feel like you could pop loose and plunge toward the void in an involuntary backflip. But if you don't get your feet high enough, they can slip off and your hands holding the crack become worthless. Either way, you're headed down.

The trick of that last hundred feet in the corner is not to let the overall pump get to you. You can't lieback forever, because the strain on your arms keeps mounting. That's what "pump" is all about. If you get too pumped, you simply can't hold on any longer.

If I'd been climbing with a rope, or even with a harness and some gear, I could always have clipped in to something, hung for a while, and regained the strength in my arms. Bad style, of course, but better than coming off. But free soloing, I had no choice. I needed to get to the top of the corner before the pump took over.

By now I was in full game-on mode, so I scurried up the corner as well as I had on toprope rehearsal. Didn't even come close to losing it. My only concession to the airiness of being up there without a rope or gear was that I cranked my feet a little higher than I had on my two toprope rehearsals. That meant more arm-pump, but it felt a bit more secure.

The three pitches above the crux are rated 5.12a, 5.12a, and 5.12b—pretty darned hard, but well within my abilities. In fact, those pitches follow a perfect finger crack. It was here that the true glory of free soloing came home to me. Sticking my first digits into the crack, I turned them slightly into perfect fingerlocks, and I felt bomber. At any given moment, I had only a tiny amount of skin inside the crack—like half of two fingers—and my toes weren't on holds, but just pasted to the wall. So little of my body was actually touching the rock. There was air all around me. I felt like I was stepping into the void, and yet it was an amazing sensation. I was one hundred percent certain I wouldn't fall off, and that certainty was what kept me from falling off.

And here, though I didn't pause to look around and take in the view, the beauty of Zion came home. The whole world of the canyon is all red and green—red for the rocks, green for the forest. There's the Virgin River winding so far below. No traffic sounds, that far up. Just peace and quiet.

A final 5.10d pitch leads to the summit, tough enough in its own right. But I climbed it as smoothly as the pitches just before. All the feelings of vague doubt I had on starting up the route had vanished.

Almost before I knew it, I stood on top of the cliff. I checked my time against the iPod. One hour and twenty-three minutes. It was the speed record, as well as the first free solo ascent.

Standing there, as I unlaced my shoes, I was superpsyched. Though I still had to hike down barefoot (rock shoes are so tight that it's excruciating to hike in them), then circle back around and wade the river again to get my approach shoes and pack (it's never smooth sailing off into the rainbow), I was totally jazzed. During that hour and twenty-three minutes, I'd climbed as well as I ever had in my life.

O N APRIL 1, 2008, no one witnessed Alex's climb of Moonlight Buttress. As with Astroman and the Rostrum, Alex had told no one what he was planning to do, though he had confided in Chris Weidner that the free solo was something he'd *like* to do sometime. Now, after the climb, he called Weidner and told him about his glorious day. Weidner told others, and the news spread like wildfire.

Because the climb had taken place on April Fools' Day, a substantial portion of the climbing cognoscenti wondered at first whether the whole thing was a joke, or even a hoax. But within days, the tide had swung in favor of Alex's veracity.

On the website Supertopo.com, climbers who understood the magnitude of the ascent weighed in. "Holy living f#ck!" wrote one. "Unreal," blogged another. "Just the thought gives me chills." There were also commenters who saluted the climb as inspirational: "Amazing accomplishment, Alex. Reading this post motivated me to push way harder today than I would have otherwise." And those who knew about Alex's previous solos of the Rostrum and Astroman tipped their caps: "That is unbelievable. . . . I would have said impossible, but since it has Alex's name on it . . . just insane." And: "Congrats on the send. . . . keep crankin'!"

On April 6, Jeff Lowe, who with Mike Weis had made the first ascent of Moonlight Buttress way back in 1971, posted on Super-topo that he had always known that the route would go free, and he had attempted to free it before Peter Croft and Johnny Woodward beat him to the prize in 1992. "But I never saw far enough into the crystal-ball," Lowe added, "to foresee Alex's inspired leap of faith. . . . Great job, Alex. Always take care, as I know you do."

Along with this encomium from one of America's stellar climbing pioneers, for the first time a larger media world, including the directors at Sender Films, sat up and took notice. A new phenom of the climbing world had emerged on the stage.

At twenty-two, Alex Honnold was just getting started.

CHAPTER **TWO**
A VERY PRIVATE HELL

Once I told Chris Weidner about Moonlight Buttress, I should have known the word would get out fast. He lives in Boulder, after all, right in the thick of the climbing scene.

I didn't anticipate, though, the explosion of postings on the Internet about the climb. I went online to check them out. My first reaction was surprise. Oh, wow, I'm in print! That's cool. Somebody had even dug up a photo of me climbing. That's my photo! I bragged to myself.

There was also, of course, the undercurrent of posters who wondered whether the free solo of Moonlight Buttress was an April Fools' joke. But one thing I've always appreciated about the climbing community, after so many of my climbs by now have gone undocumented by film or photos or unverified by witnesses, is that people have taken me at my word. In April 2008, no one on the Internet was accusing me of perpetrating a hoax. If the free solo of Moonlight Buttress was bogus, it was some poster who was lying about it—goofing on the credulity of the Supertopo audience, maybe.

I still could not have imagined ever becoming a sponsored professional climber. If I got a little notoriety, I just hoped that maybe some gear company would give me a free pair of rock shoes.

The tendinitis in my left elbow hadn't gotten any better. If anything, all the work I'd done rehearsing the moves on Moonlight Buttress and then free soloing it had probably made the condition worse.

I finally realized I had to knock off climbing for a while to let my elbow heal. That's how I ended up spending the summer in the Sierra Nevada, doing long hikes and loops on big mountains like the Evolution Traverse. It involved a lot of scrambling, but as long as I could do it in tennies, I figured it didn't count as real climbing. Meanwhile, I was getting into great shape.

Recently a journalist asked me if I could stop climbing for stretches at a time. "Sure," I answered.

"You mean you could go for, say, a month without climbing?" he asked.

"Hell, no!" I blurted out. "Not a month! I thought you meant three days."

That's just the way it is with me. No matter what else I've turned my attention to over the years, nothing seems as interesting as climbing. I can't do without it, even though by now I've been climbing in one way or another for almost twenty years straight.

That whole summer in the High Sierra, the idea of free soloing the Regular Northwest Face of Half Dome floated around inside my head. It's such an iconic formation, one of the most striking thrusts of sheer granite anywhere in North America, and I'd always loved the way it dominates the whole east end of the Valley.

By 2008, Yosemite had become my favorite climbing area in the world. Some climbers are drawn to towers and pinnacles, others to complex ridges. What I love is big, clean faces, and they don't get any better than the ones in Yosemite—especially El Capitan and Half Dome. You stand at the base of El Cap and look up its 2,700-foot precipice, and you just say, "Wow!"

Granite is also my favorite kind of rock. And that's what Yosemite is made of—more clean, sweeping walls of granite than anywhere else in North America.

The Regular Northwest Face route takes a pure line up the left-hand side of the nearly vertical wall. That summer as I got in shape making loops and traverses in the High Sierra, Half Dome became my muse, a random source of motivation that drifted through my thoughts while I strolled along one ridge after another. The notion of trying to free solo the route was intimidating, yet irresistible at the same time. In terms of sheer grandness, it would be a big step up for me—an even greater challenge than Moonlight Buttress.

THE REGULAR NORTHWEST FACE ROUTE was pioneered in 1957 by Royal Robbins, the finest American rock climber of his day, and two partners, Jerry Gallwas and Mike Sherrick. Two previous attempts, including one by Robbins, had gotten no higher than a quarter of the way up the 2,000-foot wall. The face, which inclines at an average pitch of eighty-five degrees, is intimidating in the extreme. As Steve Roper writes in *Camp 4*, the definitive history of early climbing in Yosemite, "The view upward [from the base] is overpowering. It doesn't seem possible that humans can climb such an enormous cliff with normal techniques"—i.e., ropes, pitons, and bolts.

It took the 1957 trio five days to complete the ascent, during which they pulled out all the stops: using their newly invented chrome-molybdenum pitons and expansion bolts for direct aid, lowering Robbins fifty feet so he could "pendulum" sideways across the blank granite to reach a chimney system, and enduring four bivouacs as they hung from slings and stirrups. The key pitch, led by Gallwas, involved strenuous aid on pitons and bolts that reached a "disturbingly narrow" ledge stretching across the face only 200 feet below the summit. Thank God Ledge today is one of the most famous features anywhere on American rock.

The YDS scale from 5.1 to 5.15 measures only pure difficulty, with no regard to danger. Another scale within the YDS, however, is grade ratings, which indicate the overall difficulty, danger, and required commitment of a long route on a big wall or a mountain—in short, the "seriousness" of a major ascent. Until very recently, the system ranged only from Grade I to Grade VI. A few landmark ascents in the last decade—nearly all of them in the remote ranges—have been tentatively rated as Grade VII, but by and large the pinnacle of the scale remains Grade VI.

The first Grade VI ever climbed in the United States was Robbins, Gallwas, and Sherrick's 1957 ascent of the Regular Northwest Face of Half Dome. At the time, it was matched only by a few routes in Europe.

In 1976, nineteen years after Robbins's team climbed the wall, Colorado-based climbers Art Higbee and Jim Erickson made the first free ascent of the Regular Northwest Face route, eliminating all the aid moves—almost. (It was Erickson's tenth try to free climb the route.) Roped together, belaying every pitch, using pitons, nuts, and bolts for protection, the duo required thirty-four hours of extreme climbing to reach a point only one hundred feet short of the summit. There, to their chagrin, they had to resort to aid to surmount the final obstacle. That glitch rendered the deed a "magnificent failure" in Higbee's and Erickson's eyes, but subsequent climbers, impressed by the achievement, have granted them the first free ascent. Higbee and Erickson rated the climb solid 5.12—close to the highest level of technical difficulty accomplished at the time anywhere in the world. The single passage on which they had to resort to aid would also prove to be the dramatic crux of Alex's 2008 climb.

By 2008, no one had ever attempted to free solo a Grade VI climb, let alone succeeded on one.

That September, my elbow seemed healed, and I was in top shape from all that cruising around the High Sierra. Dwelling on Half Dome for months had put me in a mental state where I felt I had to do it. Maybe I'd just spent so much time thinking about it that now I had to clear it from my mind.

I'd climbed the route five or six times before with different partners, but I'd freed all the moves, roped up and clipping pro in case I fell, only twice—most recently two days before my solo attempt, when I'd gone up there with Brad Barlage. There are three completely blank sections on the route that Robbins's team solved by going on aid as they drilled bolt ladders through the impasses. Almost everybody climbs the bolt ladders today—they're secure, and relatively easy for aid. But free variations have been worked out that bypass those blank sections. That's why it's possible to climb the whole route free, as Higbee and Erickson (almost) did, though they were roped up and using pro.

After Brad and I climbed the route on September 4, I spent the whole next day resting, sitting by myself in my van, thinking about the route. I was still somewhat conflicted about going up there alone: Do I really want to do this? I'd already made plans with different friends to climb a few days later in the Valley, so I felt some pressure to get my soloing done before any of them showed up. Ultimately I decided to go back up to the base of Half Dome the next day. I told myself that I could just hike back down if I wasn't psyched. I've done that a few times, or even started a route and then backed off. In 2006, on Royal Arches Terrace, a long climb in the Valley but technically a pretty easy one, I climbed a pitch and a half up the friction slab at the start of the route, then realized I just wasn't into it. I downclimbed, hiked back to the road, and hitchhiked out of Yosemite. I was done for the season.

This time, though, I knew that once I got up to the base of Half Dome, there was no way I was going to bail.

I didn't want to make a big fuss about my project, so I told only two people about it, Brad and Chris Weidner. Brad said, "What the fuck?" But then, "Okay, be safe. Text me when you're done." He was being a bro.

Chris tried to talk me out of it. "Dude, that's crazy," he said. "You should rehearse the hell out of it on a toprope before you try to solo it."

"Nah," I answered. "I want to keep it sporting."

"Are you crazy?"

When I look back on those exchanges, it sounds as though I was being flippant or arrogant. That's not what was going on. I just didn't want to make too big a deal about the attempt—especially in case I backed off low on the route. It's bad form to brag about a climb before you do it. And I didn't want my good buddies to get too alarmed—then I might start worrying about them worrying about me! I guess I was just trying to reassure them: Hey, guys, I think I can handle this. I'll be safe.

There was something else going on as well. Despite my emphasis on methodical preparation, I'd begun to think that maybe I'd rehearsed the moves on Moonlight Buttress so thoroughly that I actually took some of the challenge out of the climb. Half Dome was so much bigger than Moonlight that it would take forever to get all the moves dialed. I decided to head up the wall with a little less preparation—that's what I meant by "keeping it sporting."

As it would turn out, maybe too sporting. . . .

In September it's still pretty hot in the Valley. That meant there weren't likely to be many other climbers on the face, which is what I was hoping for. But because the wall faces northwest, in September it stays in shade the whole day, which meant I could climb without getting too sweaty or dehydrated. Sweaty hands make smooth climbing pretty dicey, no matter how much you chalk up, and dehydration not only saps your strength but also can interfere with your judgment.

So on September 6, I found myself at the base of the route again. With a much lighter load than I'd carried with Brad two days before, the approach hike had taken far less time, but the whole way I felt the face looming over me. I tried not to think about it too much. It was a bluebird day, a perfect, clear morning. Resting at the base, I felt completely detached from the rest of the Valley glowing in the morning sun below me. As I had hoped, I had the whole wall entirely to myself. For the next few hours I would be alone in a unique way, locked in a high-stakes game of solitude.

It's not much trouble to climb through a roped party when you're soloing—I'd done it before, and I'd do it again. But encountering others on the wall, especially if they express their incredulity that you're climbing without a rope, can make you self-conscious. And that can interfere with the absolute concentration you need to pull off a big free solo. Before such a climb, I have to get really psyched up. And once I'm off the ground, I'm totally fixated. I'm going to do this. It's the most important thing in life right now. That's not the kind of mental state I can share with random strangers.

I was wearing only shorts and a long-sleeved T-shirt. I had my Miura rock shoes on my feet, and my chalk bag dangling at my back, but no harness, and not even a single carabiner. In one pocket I put a few Clif Kid Zbars, my favorite multi-pitch snack, and I filled a collapsible flask with about a third of a liter of water. I put that in my other pocket, though it pulled my shorts down a little. But I knew it would take me a few hours to climb the route, and I didn't want to be parched by the time I reached the hard pitches up high. A pack was out of the question, partly because of all the chimneys in the middle of the route (it's almost impossible to chimney wearing a pack), but mainly because the climbing was hard enough that I didn't want any extra weight on my body.

Finally, there was nothing else for me to do but quit procrastinating and climb. I started up the first pitch.

•   •   •   •

For years, the great Yosemite pioneers had been heroes of a sort to me. The guys from the "golden age" of the 1960s—Royal Robbins, Warren Harding, Yvon Chouinard, Tom Frost, Chuck Pratt, and the like—were almost too remote in history for me to appreciate, even though I'd read stories about their memorable antics. It was the self-described Stonemasters of the next generation, in the 1970s and '80s, that I most admired. John Long, Jim Bridwell, Billy Westbay, Tobin Sorenson, and their buddies. . . . But especially John Bachar and Peter Croft, because of their soloing and free climbing at the highest level. And Lynn Hill, the first person, male or female, to climb the Nose route on El Capitan completely free, in 1993. A year later, she freed the route in a single day. Those are still two of the greatest feats ever pulled off in the Valley. I was also fascinated by John "Yabo" Yablonski, to whom so many wild and crazy stories clung—about him falling off a free solo and saving himself by catching a tree branch, about his nude ascent of North Overhang, about his infamous "screamers" when he fell (roped) as far as a hundred feet, only to be caught by miracle belays. Yabo was evidently a tortured soul, for he committed suicide in the early 1990s.

A lot of the Stonemasters, though, were into drugs. Some of them even bragged about doing serious climbs in Yosemite while they were tripping their brains out on LSD. Their style was part of the counterculture movement of the day, but I just couldn't relate to it. I've never done drugs, and though I've tasted alcohol, I've never had a whole drink. I don't even drink coffee. I had a small cup once—it was like drinking battery acid. I had to poop all morning. I once had a sniff of Scotch. I thought, I should be cleaning my sink with this stuff. It's not some moral objection—drugs and booze and caffeine just have no appeal to me.

I grew up in Sacramento, California. Both my parents taught English as a Second Language (ESL) at a series of institutions in the United States and abroad. Eventually they landed more permanent jobs at American River College in Sacramento. My mom, Dierdre Wolownick, taught ESL, Spanish, and French at the college. Today she constitutes the entire French department for the school. She's a gifted linguist, fluent in three foreign languages (French, Spanish, and Italian) and competent in German, Polish, Japanese, and a bit of American Sign Language.

My dad, Charles Honnold, got a full-time job teaching ESL at American River College before my mom did. So I grew up in an intellectual, academic climate—for whatever good that did me.

Mom likes to tell people that on the day I was born, August 17, 1985, I could stand up, holding onto her fingers. Like a lot of her stories about me as a kid, I tend to think she made that up—or at least stretched the truth pretty far. She's told journalists that from the time I was two years old, she knew I'd become a climber. She also relates a story about taking me to a climbing gym when I was only five. According to Mom, she was talking to the supervisor, turned around, and found me thirty feet up in only a minute or two. She says she was scared to death I'd kill myself.

My sister, Stasia, was born two years before me. From our infancy on, Mom spoke only French to us. Her idea was to make us bilingual. She still speaks only French to us when we visit. But Stasia and I rebelled from the start—we'd answer her in English. Even so, I'll have to give Mom the credit for making me pretty fluent in French. My grasp of the language has come in handy on many trips to France and three to North Africa.

Mom may be right about me being an uncontrollable, hyper

little monster. At age five or six, I broke my arm for the first time. I'd decided it would be fun to run down the slide at Carl's Jr.—my favorite restaurant. I went over the edge. The docs called it a green twig radius fracture, whatever that is.

I broke my arm a second time at age seven or eight. This was a really pitiful accident—in fact, it's hard to describe how I fucked up. There was a big rope that was part of a play structure in our backyard. It was meant be a rope swing, but I rigged it as a tight-rope, then lay down on it as if it were a hammock. Fell off and broke my arm.

Dad took me to the local climbing gym when I was ten. It was just a random stab at another kind of recreation, but it "took" from the first day. For years thereafter, he would drive me to the gym and spend the whole afternoon belaying me—he wasn't interested in climbing himself. Later he even drove me to other gyms around California where I'd enter competitions.

He was a man of very few words. We'd drive for hours with almost no conversation. He wasn't comfortable expressing his emotions, but belaying me tirelessly and driving me all over the state was his own way of showing love.

From childhood on, there was an elephant in the room. It was that my parents weren't happily married. They didn't fight openly—it was more just a kind of chilly silence that filled the house. For Stasia's and my sake, they waited till after I graduated from high school to get a divorce. But we knew they were going to split up, because we occasionally read Mom's e-mails. The real bummer for them was that they were so much happier after they got divorced, and they stayed friends.

I'm sure a shrink would have a field day with the fact that, to this day, I have a hard time remembering the details of my child-hood. In 2011, when Alex Lowther interviewed me for a profile for Alpinist, he started quizzing me about the early years. I told him *that my memories were fuzzy and unreliable. "Ask Ben about this stuff," I said. Ben Smalley and I had been best friends since first grade.*

L OWTHER DID JUST AS Alex suggested, contacting Smalley, who by 2011 had become an air force lieutenant. Smalley's sardonic portrait of Alex as a kid and teenager rounds out the picture of the dorky misfit Alex genuinely considered himself, even after he started to attract the notice of the climbing world. According to Smalley, as told to Lowther,

> Alex wore sweatpants to school. Every day. There was a gray pair and a blue pair. He wore T-shirts that were two sizes too big, and they said things on them like, "I hiked the Grand Canyon," "Visit Yellowstone," or "How to Identify Deer Tracks." He was very good at capture the flag. Defensively. He could talk to you about the War of 1812 for an hour. It wasn't so much that he was shy, as he just didn't even bother to try. Like, he would speak to you if you spoke to him. He wore hoodies in class, always with the hood up, and he would just sit there, but he always knew the answer if a teacher called on him. He's got sort of a Holden Caulfield thing going on, maybe, in that he's always on the lookout for a phony.

When that passage was read out loud to Alex, he confessed, "Ben's got me down." All the details about his youthful persona, Alex confirmed. The passage stirred up other memories. "I still love sweats," he said. "I never wear jeans." And: "I had another T-shirt from Banff or Jasper, with a picture of a bear on it, but a bear with antlers. It read, 'I am not a bear.' It was part of some kind of don't-feed-the-bears campaign.

"About the War of 1812—my dad gave me a book about decisive battles in history. The *Monitor* and the *Merrimack*, Hannibal crossing the Alps, that kind of thing. I loved history. It wasn't that I hated school—just that I was an uncool kid. I had a hard time talking to strangers."

In Lowther's profile, Smalley went on:

His parents were not very happily married. His father would sit on the couch most nights, reading until he fell asleep. I would say [Alex] got worse in high school, actually. He withdrew further. He hung out with the kids who played Pokémon in the math room at lunch. During sophomore year, Alex got his first girlfriend. Her name was Elizabeth Thomas. She went by E.T. That should give you some idea of the social circle she ran in. I just don't think Alex thought the typical high school stuff was for him. He considered himself more of a loner.

Says Alex, "E.T. was cool. Ben didn't like her. She was half-Irish, half-Japanese. A nice girl, real smart. We were a couple for maybe three years."

In high school, Alex consistently scored high marks, finishing with a weighted grade-point average of 4.8. Yet he wasn't at all sure he wanted to go to college. At the last minute, he applied only to two branches of the University of California—at Davis and Berkeley. Accepted by both, he chose Berkeley.

The single year he spent at one of the elite bastions of higher learning was, Alex feels now, a waste of time. "I had vague plans to major in engineering," he says. "But I didn't make any friends at Berkeley. I can't recall a single student or a single professor. I should have lived in a dorm, instead of the two-bedroom apartment a friend of our family let me sublet. I spent a year basically in isolation.

"I did have a job as a security guard. For fourteen dollars an hour,

I'd walk around by myself all night. I had a police radio. Sometimes I'd escort girls back to their dorms.

"The second semester, I stopped going to classes. I'd buy a loaf of bread and an apple and go out to Indian Rock"—a diminutive crag in the suburban Berkeley Hills—"and do laps. I just couldn't hack college." That summer, like most freshmen, he moved back home with his mother.

Alex's parents' divorce became final in May of his freshman year. Two months later, on July 18, his father was rushing through the Phoenix airport, trying to make a tight connection, when he dropped dead of a heart attack. Alex got the news when he came home from a long hike. He recalled the event to Alex Lowther:

> The house was open, all the windows were open and stuff, but like, everything was dark; nobody was in the house. And, I was like, "Mom?"—"Mom?" And went and found Mom sitting outside in the pool. Sitting with her legs in the pool. Just sitting there crying. And she was just like, "Your dad died." I don't remember what she said, but basically like, "Your dad died," and then she went to bed.
>
> I don't remember disbelieving her. But for all I knew, he could still be alive. I never saw a body. There was never a real funeral. This little can of ashes showed up one day, and people said he was dead. I read all the articles about him. For a while I would see people on the bike path. People who looked like Dad, with a big beard and just all big, and I would be like, "Oh!" And then, "Oh, that wasn't him."

Ben Smalley told Lowther, "I kind of had to yell at him about it. 'Why aren't you upset?' I think deep down, Alex never did any mourning."

"Did you mourn at all?" Lowther asked Alex.

"I was too young and angstful," he answered. "I had too much anger."

Alex clarifies: "It wasn't that I didn't believe Mom when she told me Dad had died. It's that my family doesn't do funerals. Dad was cremated in Phoenix. There was a memorial service at Lake Tahoe. I thought, 'Huh, I'll never see him again.' But there was no closure."

Charles Honnold was fifty-five when he died. Alex was nineteen. The event crystallized Alex's decision to drop out of Berkeley. Supported by the interest from his father's life insurance bonds, he "borrowed" his mother's minivan and set out for various California crags and the life of a dirtbag climber. In 2007, he bought a used Ford Econoline van that he converted into a cozy garret-on-wheels. Eight years later, after many home improvements, and despite his fame and unexpected wealth, Alex still lives in the van. His default residence is his mother's house in Sacramento, where he spends a few weeks each year.

Whether or not he truly mourned his father's death, the loss had a profound impact on Alex's outlook on life. His mother's parents had been devout Catholics, and both Stasia and Alex attended Catholic services when they were young. The effect was to turn Alex into a confirmed atheist. As he sardonically commented in a 2012 YouTube video, "At no point did I ever think there was ever anything going on with church. I always saw it as a bunch of old people eating stale wafers. . . ."

His father's death brought home the *carpe diem* injunction to live the only life he has to the fullest. In a 2012 Q&A for *National Geographic Adventure*, Alex came up with a startling metaphor. He was asked, "If you don't believe in God or an after-life, doesn't that make this life all the more precious?"

Alex responded: "I suppose so, but just because something is precious doesn't mean you have to baby it. Just like suburbanites who have a shiny new SUV that they are afraid to dent. What's the point in having an amazing vehicle if you're afraid to drive it?

"I'm trying to take my vehicle to new and interesting places. And I try my very best not to crash, but at least I take it out."

The Regular Northwest Face route on Half Dome begins with a 5.10c finger crack that happens to be one of my favorite pitches on the whole climb. The next two pitches are only 5.9 and 5.8. It was a good warm-up for the two thousand feet of climbing above me.

But then, on what's normally the fourth pitch, I ran into the first bolt ladder. There are two variations that bypass that blank section on either side. I'd climbed first one, then the other, on my two roped free climbs of the route. On the left is the two-pitch Higbee 'Hedral, rated a stern 5.12a, first freed by Art Higbee on his 1976 ascent with Jim Erickson. On the right is the Huber 'Hedral, named after the German climber Alex Huber, full-on 5.11d. ('Hedral is slang for "dihedral," a vertical inside corner in the rock. Thanks to Art and Alex for the handy alliteration of their last names!)

Even though the Huber variation is one grade easier, it's less secure. You have to traverse across a wall that's so smooth it's like polished glass. I thought about what it would take, then told myself, Screw that, and chose the Higbee 'Hedral instead.

The crux 5.12a sequence comes in a short boulder problem off a big, comfortable ledge. It made, I thought, for secure soloing, since if I couldn't connect the moves I thought I could jump off and land on the ledge. But those are some of the hardest moves on the whole route, and I had to shift my mentality from cruising up fun cracks to actually cranking on small holds. I laced my shoes up extra tight, then powered through the six-move boulder problem without hesitating.

The rest of the pitch was quite dirty. Half Dome is so much

higher in altitude than the other walls in the Valley that it has some of the feel of an alpine mountain. And with mountains, you get loose holds that you have to test before pulling on them. (Pulling loose a single hold, obviously, can spell the difference between life and death when you're free soloing.) You also get dirt and even vegetation in the cracks. Because the free variations are tackled so seldom, they don't get "gardened" by climbers the way the regular pitches do. It's a scary business to be on rock that ought to be reasonable to climb, only to have your fingers scraping through wet dirt or your toes jammed on clumps of moss or scrawny little shrubs.

But I followed the faint trail of chalk marks that Brad and I had left two days earlier, and managed to avoid most of the vegetation and dirt. As I rejoined the normal route, I relaxed and mentally shifted gears back into cruise mode. I had about a thousand feet of climbing above me until I got to the next hard pitch. I wanted to go slow and steady, so as not to get tired. A slow jog, rather than a sprint.

I had my iPod with headband ear buds so I could listen to tunes while I climbed. When the going got harder, I'd knock one earbud out. If it was really serious, both buds, so I wouldn't be distracted. The headband then would just dangle from my neck. That day I was cycling through some songs by Eminem, especially "Lose Yourself."

The beautiful day was holding steady, but I had no time to look around and admire the scenery. Scenery is what you get to enjoy when you're belaying your partner on a conventional roped climb. When I'm free soloing, even on the easier pitches, I'm totally focused on what's in front of me. The universe shrinks down to me and the rock. You don't take a single hold for granted.

The sheer magnitude of the wall came home to me as I climbed. I realized that this project was way more serious than Moonlight Buttress, even though both routes are rated 5.12.

Pretty soon I was halfway up the route, a thousand feet off the deck. Here the line, as first climbed in 1957, suddenly traverses to

the right to access an enormous chimney system. The final section
of blank rock before the chimney is normally tackled by a fifty-foot
bolt ladder. The previous time I'd free climbed the route, I circum-
vented the bolt ladder via a 5.12c pitch, using the bolts for protection but not aid. But now as I was approaching the ladder, I got
cold feet about soloing it. The pitch is extremely insecure: slopers
and scoops, shallow indentations you can barely hold with flat-
tened fingers, and which you have to "smear" with your feet, strain-
ing your ankles so that you can get as much friction as possible on
the holds with the soles of your shoes. Then those moves are followed by a down mantle. It's a tricky move, like lowering yourself
off a table with your hands extended downward, palms gripping
the edge of the ledge. Balance is everything, and it's hard to look
down to see where to place your feet. And the feet have to find a
narrow ridge of granite on which you step before you can let go of
the mantle and move on.

The free variation Higbee and Erickson worked out in 1976
breaks off to the left a pitch before the bolt ladder and circles
around this whole section of the wall, rejoining the route another
pitch above. I'd never climbed it, and I'd heard that it was loose
and dirty, but suddenly adventurous 5.10 seemed a lot more fun
than insecure 5.12c. The variation is a pretty devious line, as you
climb a long 5.9 gully straight up, followed by a meandering 5.10b
scuttle toward the right, after which you have to downclimb a hundred feet of 5.10 to get into the chimney system.

I broke off the normal route at a random point and started wandering upward, trying to find the 5.10 variation. But as I moved,
I started to get confused about the line. The bushes I was climbing through gave me pause. There were no real signs of human
presence here—no chalk marks from previous climbers, no fixed
pitons, or even scars where they might have once been driven and
removed. I started to worry that I was completely dropping the

ball. I was literally in the center of Half Dome, a thousand feet off the ground, possibly off-route, on dirt.

I said to myself, Holy shit! This is hardcore. I hope I can find my way back. It wasn't true panic that I felt—just an uncomfortable anxiety. It would have helped a lot if I had climbed this variation before. But I guessed this is what I'd bargained for when I told Chris Weidner I wanted to keep the challenge "sporting."

· · · ·

Fear. It's the most primal element in cutting-edge climbing, or indeed, in adventure of any kind. Even nonclimbers can recognize that fact, when they watch footage of me free soloing. That's why the first question out of their mouths is usually, "Aren't you afraid . . . ?" (They don't have to finish the sentence—"that you're going to die?")

I've done a lot of thinking about fear. For me, the crucial question is not how to climb without fear—that's impossible—but how to deal with it when it creeps into your nerve endings.

Interviewed later by Sender Films, my Valley buddy Nick Martino claimed, "Honnold's on another level than anyone else out there. It's like he doesn't feel fear or any of the normal emotions that anybody else feels. He has this ability to just shut his brain off and do the sickest climbs that have ever been done."

Thanks, Nick, but that just isn't true. I feel fear just like the next guy. If there was an alligator nearby that was about to eat me, I'd feel pretty uncomfortable. In fact, the two worst doses of fear I've experienced in my life so far—both the result of heinous misadventures that sprang from seemingly minor mistakes—didn't come when I was free soloing. If I learned anything from those two screwups, it's never to take for granted even a casual outing in the backcountry.

It was the day after Christmas, 2004. I was nineteen. My dad had died five months before, so I decided to hike up an easy peak that had been a favorite destination for both of us—Mount Tallac near Lake Tahoe. It's all of 9,739 feet above sea level, but it rises a respectable 3,250 feet from its base. I'd climbed it a ton of times, but never in winter. We had actually scattered some of Dad's ashes on the summit the previous summer, shortly after he died.

In Dad's closet, I found an old pair of snowshoes. I'd never snowshoed before—never even done much of anything in the snow. As it turned out, they weren't very good snowshoes for this sort of outing—they didn't have crampons attached to the webbing. But I didn't know any better.

As it also turns out, the snow had fallen about a month before, and it had been dry ever since. So the snow had turned to a hard, icy crust.

I didn't want to take the slower, circuitous normal trail, with its ups and downs, so I just headed up one of the couloirs. I was tramping along, but the surface underfoot really sucked. And there was a crazy wind that day. I got most of the way up the couloir before I said to myself, This is bad. I tried to turn around to descend, and I just slipped.

I remember sliding down the hill, whipping out of control. I went at least several hundred feet. I had time to think, Oh my God, I'm going to die!

I came to in the rocks. I'd been knocked out cold, whether for mere seconds or for longer, I couldn't tell. I think I must have hit the rocks with my feet, then rag-dolled over and crushed my face. I had a broken hand. I thought my leg was broken, but it turned out it was just badly bruised. I had a punctured sinus cavity in my face and several chipped teeth. I'd been wearing gloves, but the thumbs had torn off—I must have been trying to self-arrest with my hands. The skin on my thumbs was like raw meat, as if they'd been sliced with a carrot peeler.

My mom had given me a cell phone for Christmas. I got it out and managed to call her. I don't remember this, but Mom later claimed my first words were, "Who am I? Where am I? What am I doing?" Mom called 911.

The normal rescue helicopter couldn't get in to where I had fallen, so they brought in a California Highway Patrol chopper. It took a while. Pretty soon I was lucid again. I could see lakes in the distance that I recognized. But I was still asking myself, "Why am I here?"

I must have been in shock. All the fear had occupied those few seconds of whipping down the icy slope, in the form of sheer terror and the conviction that I was about to die, but now I felt a deeper sort of dread: How badly am I hurt? Am I going to get out of here all right?

There was an Indian family out snowshoeing who came along from below. Two strapping twenty-five-year-old lads and their parents. They helped load me into the chopper. Within minutes I was in an emergency room in Reno. It would take months for me to fully recover, especially because I kept climbing while my broken hand was healing. I still have scar tissue on my right thumb where the skin was scraped off.

This is still the only real accident I've suffered. And what a complete debacle it was, thanks to my ignorance of snow and snowshoes. If this happened today, I'd be mortified. But I'd also self-assess, then hike out under my own steam. It's embarrassing to have to be rescued by helicopter. When I tell the story today, now that I've done so much serious climbing, the only way to treat it is as comedy. Maybe farce.

I'd started keeping my climbing "bible" the previous month. That day, writing left-handed because I'd broken my right hand, I recorded

Tallac

Fell, broke hand . . . airlifted.

Should have stayed more calm and walked off. Pussy.

• • • •

The most scared I've ever gotten while climbing came when I was twenty-one, a couple of years after my snowshoe fiasco. I was with my second serious girlfriend, Mandi (short for Amanda) Finger. She was a solid 5.13 climber I'd met at Jailhouse Rock, a sport-climbing crag near Sonora. She was five or six years older than me, but we hit it off. We climbed together at Joshua Tree and Red Rocks near Las Vegas. We even talked about going to Europe.

Anyway, on this particular day we decided to climb a three-pitch 5.12 route called the Nautilus, in the Needles, a range of granite spires near the Kern River. The routes are trad climbs with the occasional bolt anchor. The Needles as a whole have a well-earned reputation for being intimidating.

The Nautilus is actually on the east face of a formation called the Witch. It takes a long and tricky approach, winding between and around other towers, then scrambling up to the base, just to get to the start of the route.

I led the whole way. The first pitch is a classic 5.12b. I climbed it in style, thinking, "Ah, sweet!" According to the topo, or route diagram, that I had with me, the next pitch was 11+, followed by a 5.10 finish. I didn't have any major trouble with the second pitch, but at the top I saw that the bolt anchors were way out in space, on the blank wall to the right, away from the crack system I'd climbed. It looked like a 5.11 traverse just to get to the anchors to clip in and belay.

So I said, Screw that. I'll just keep going. Combine the third pitch with the second in one long lead. I had a seventy-meter rope, so I figured it would reach.

What I didn't know was that the last pitch was loaded with loose, refrigerator-size stones that you had to lieback past—"death blocks," as climbers call them. We were in shade, it was cold, and by now I'd developed serious rope drag from all the bends in the rope as it linked the pieces of pro I'd placed on the previous pitch. There I was, doing strenuous liebacking, trying not to dislodge any of the death blocks, and the rope drag was making it really hard to pull up any slack. On top of that, I couldn't get in any protection, as I'd used up most of my rack on the third pitch. All I had left was a Black Alien—the smallest cam anybody manufactures—a few nuts, and three carabiners.

The climbing just felt too hard. No way it was 5.10. Later I found another topo that rated the last pitch at 11+. Basically, I was getting gripped—grasping the holds too hard out of fear and uncertainty.

Mandi had been stuck in her belay way below me for about an hour. Now she yelled up encouraging comments, like, "I'm cold! I'm scared! Can we go down?"

If I could have gotten in an anchor to rappel off, I probably would have gone down. Instead, I kept fighting my way upward. I placed no pro in the last forty or fifty feet. If I came off there, I'd take a really long, bad fall, with all those big blocks to worry about pulling loose or cutting the rope. The dread was mounting. I was seriously scared.

The last pitch ends in a little roof that caps the whole route. I got to just below the roof, but here the rock turned all licheny and dirty. The rope drag was horrible. There was a last mantle move to get over the roof, but I couldn't figure out which way to do it. At last I found a crack to get the Black Alien in, and I just busted for the top. I did a really hard move, a full-on iron cross, crimping on tiny holds.

It was so fucked. As I sat on top, belaying Mandi, I had only one meter of rope left. I'd used up the other sixty-nine linking the last two pitches. And I could barely pull up the rope, the drag was so bad.

That's the most frightened I've ever been climbing, and it came not on a free solo but on a conventional roped climb. All because of an impulsive decision to skip the bolt anchor and an ignorance of just how difficult the top pitch was.

Today, I would have handled the whole thing better. I've got more tools in my tool kit now. Maybe I could have downclimbed, or placed less pro on the second pitch so I had more left for the finish.

But as I sat there, emotionally exhausted, hauling the heavy rope that was tied to Mandi, I thought I was ready to give up climbing for good. Maybe I should go back to college, I said to myself, and finish my education.

Of course, by the very next day, everything seemed different. I wasn't about to give up climbing. I'd just make sure to avoid getting stuck in cul-de-sacs like that last pitch on the Nautilus.

Easier said than done.

• • • •

On September 6, 2008, a thousand feet up the Regular Northwest Face of Half Dome, as I pushed through dirty cracks and vegetation, wondering if I'd gotten off route on the Higbee-Erickson free variation, I sensed the threat of another cul-de-sac. My anxiety wasn't ratcheted up to the level of genuine fear, but it got my attention. So I focused hard, took a deep breath, and sorted out my options.

I told myself it wasn't a do-or-die situation. Climbing down is almost always harder than climbing up, but I still felt that I could have downclimbed the whole route so far, all thousand feet of it, if I had to. For that matter, if I got into a truly nasty predicament, I could always sit and wait, even for a day or two, until some other climbers came along, ask to tie in with them, and finish the climb as their probably unwelcome guest. "Hitchhiking," I call it. Other climbers in Yosemite have chosen that means of escape, or even have had to be rescued by helicopter, but I've never had to resort to either gambit, thank God—except for my ignominious chopper rescue on Mount Tallac, but that wasn't climbing. On Half Dome, "hitchhiking" would have really sucked, and a helicopter rescue would have been even worse.

As I later realized, I had climbed too high before traversing right. For all I know, on that traverse I was inventing a new variation to the Higbee-Erickson free variation, charting new waters. The variation is supposed to end with a hundred-foot downclimb of a 5.10 finger crack. I actually had to downclimb 150 feet. Eventually, though, I found some old nylon slings hanging from pitons, and that bolstered my confidence. But then I found it hard to get my fat fingers into the 5.10 crack. I could only lodge the first knuckle in a crack where other climbers—Lynn Hill, for example—could have sunk all three knuckles on each finger. So the downclimb felt distressingly "thin," harder than 5.10, and the pitch took me a long time. In all, the variation cost me a ton of time—in actuality, maybe fifteen minutes, though it seemed an eternity—and a lot of stress, and I was relieved to finally get back onto the clean, well-traveled path.

I put on my headband iPod again and switched back into auto-pilot mode for the next five hundred feet of chimney climbing. It felt great to be in a clean, secure chimney. A pleasant routine of squirming my back, stemming my feet, palming, and repeating for hundreds of feet. I took it slow and steady, enjoying the climbing. And that brought me to Big Sandy, an enormous ledge system 1,600 feet up the wall.

So far, I'd eaten none of my food and drunk none of my water. Big Sandy isn't the only place on the route where you can sit down, but it's such a spacious ledge you could have a barbecue there with friends (if you could get them up there in the first place). I spent a few minutes taking off my shoes and relaxing. It had taken me about two hours of climbing to get here, and now I needed a breather. I ate my bars and drank the water, so I wouldn't have to carry the weight through the next hard pitches. Some climbers might have tossed the plastic flask once it was empty, but I've always believed in packing out your trash, so I stuck it back in my pocket. Soon enough, I retightened my shoes, set my iPod to repeat Eminem, and started climbing again.

The day was getting warmer, even though I was still in shadow. At some point I took off my shirt and wrapped it around my waist, cinching it with an over-and-under tuck of the sleeves. My short rest stop hadn't really felt like relief, because I knew the hardest part of the climb was still above me. That final challenge hung over me the whole time I sat on Big Sandy, ramping up my concentration and intensity for the crux to come.

Resting can be a double-edged sword. When you're free soloing, the pain in your feet and your fatigue just seem to vanish. When you rest, those annoyances come back. You have to snap out of it and get serious again.

The next three pitches above Big Sandy are called the Zig-Zags, presumably for the single, zigzagging crack/corner system they follow. Rated 5.11d, 5.10b, and 5.11c, they've always seemed harder to me. Maybe it's because I happen to have huge fingers, but the thin crack set in a steep, polished corner has always felt more like 5.12. Aesthetically, the Zig-Zags represent the best Yosemite has to offer, perfect clean corners with staggering exposure. But I wasn't thinking about the amazing view of the Valley as I carefully liebacked my way up the first tenuous pitch.

I climbed almost in a daze. I knew what to do; I just tried not to think about it too much. I didn't think about the next hard pitches *above. I didn't think about the 5.11+ slab on top, a pitch above the Zig-Zags. I just moved steadily between small fingerlocks up the steep dihedral. The crux of the first Zig-Zag felt much easier than it had two days before, probably because now I had the sequence dialed. Every hold felt crisp and perfect, and I pulled really hard.*

The second pitch of the Zig-Zags flew by in a frenzy of hand jams and hero liebacking. The climbing was secure enough that I could relax and enjoy it. With every zag of the crack, I found myself handjamming over big protruding blocks, the base of the wall almost 2,000 feet below me, the Valley floor itself 4,000 feet below. The pitch was a delight, compared to the thin liebacks above and below.

Handjamming is another essential technique for the rock climber, and it's surprising that it took many decades to invent. If a vertical crack is between about two and five inches wide, but there are no edges inside it to grasp with the fingers, you can still use it for a hold, by inserting the whole hand, then flexing it to fit the crack, either by making a fist or by arching the back of the hand against the straightened fingers. Your hand acts like a wedge that you can put your whole weight on. Jamming is tough on the knuckles, and guys bent on a hard day of crack climbing will tape their hands to minimize the damage. I've never been into tape myself, though, mainly because my skin is so naturally resilient— I don't tend to suffer from the little cuts and scrapes that other climbers do.

I stopped again for a minute below the last Zig-Zag. I felt good but wanted to be sure I didn't get pumped. On a rope, you're forced to rest at least fifteen minutes per pitch while you belay. But when you solo, you never have to stop, so I force myself to pause at stances and relax, just to make sure I don't get ahead of myself. After a two-minute breather, I set out up the undercling lieback feature, a slight variation on the original aid line. The undercling is somewhat pumpy but only 5.11c, not terribly difficult compared to the original corner, which is supposedly 5.12+ (though I've never tried it). The real crux of the variation is making blind gear placements in the flaring crack. But since I wasn't placing gear, I was doing the pitch the "easy way."

Still, it was another pitch of insecure liebacking, with both feet pasted against a smooth granite wall and flared jams for my fingers. Again, as on the whole rest of the route, the crux of the pitch was an extra-thin section. I knew exactly what to do and hurried through it. The nearly two thousand feet of climbing below me were beginning to take their toll. I was finding it harder and harder to give the climbing my complete attention. Part of me just wanted to get the climb over with.

With the last Zig-Zag below me, I was soon walking across Thank God Ledge, the amazing sliver of rock that traverses out from beneath the Visor, only about 200 feet shy of the summit. I could hear noises from above and knew lots of people would be up top on this perfect late summer morning. The easy Cable route up the other side of Half Dome is one of the most popular hikes in the Valley, culminating in a fifty-five-degree slab on which the National Park Service has installed a pair of metal cords to use like handrails. On a warm sunny day like this one, there's a nonstop procession of hikers lined up on the cables like airport travelers in a taxi queue.

I could hear the chatter of the tourists on top, but no heads peered over the edge. I was glad no one was watching.

I walked across Thank God Ledge as a matter of pride. I had walked its thirty-five-foot length before, but I'd also crawled or hand-traversed it. It's less than a foot wide at its narrowest, with the wall above bulging ever so slightly at one point. But I didn't want to taint my solo ascent—I had to do this correctly. (Incidentally, walking Thank God Ledge is another of those things that's quite a bit easier with no harness, rope, gear, or pack hanging off you. The balance is more natural.) The first few steps were completely normal, as if I was walking on a narrow sidewalk in the sky. But once it narrowed, I found myself inching along, facing out with my body glued to the wall, shuffling my feet and maintaining perfect posture. I could have looked down and seen my pack sitting at the base of the route 1,800 feet below, but it would have pitched me headfirst off the wall. The ledge ends at a short squeeze chimney that guards the beginning of the final slab to the summit.

I paused for a moment beneath the ninety-foot slab, looked up to see if anyone was watching (still no one), and started up. The first few moves are easy enough, on somewhat positive holds with good feet. As you get higher, the holds disappear and the feet shrink. Two days earlier, I'd considered two sections "cruxy." The first involved a step-through onto a miserly smear, while the second, thirty feet higher, involved a few moves of shitty hands and feet before reaching a "jug"—a big, positive edge I could wrap my fingers around that marked the end of the hard climbing, sixty feet up the pitch.

I also knew that it was this slab that had thwarted Higbee and Erickson's attempt to climb the whole route free. So close to the summit, they'd had to use aid to surmount the last obstacle. Perhaps that should have given me pause.

I hardly noticed the first crux. I cruised right through it, feeling pretty good about myself. Twenty feet of thin cord hung from one of the bolts. I very briefly considered running the cord under my thumb—not weighting it but having it there just in case. But that felt suspiciously like cheating.

I climbed into the upper crux, feeling good about doing things legit. And then I ground to a halt. I'd expected to find some sort of different hold or sequence from the one I'd used two days earlier, which had felt pretty desperate, but perhaps I'd done it wrong. This time, in the same position on the same holds, I realized there were no better options. I had a moment of doubt . . . or maybe panic. It was hard to tell which. Although I'd freed the pitch maybe two other times the year before, I could remember nothing of the sequence or holds, perhaps because there aren't any.

A gigantic old oval carabiner hung from a bolt about two inches above the pathetic ripple that was my right handhold. I alternated back and forth, chalking up my right hand and then my left, switching feet on marginal smears to shake out my calves. I couldn't make myself commit to the last terrible right-foot smear I needed to snag the jug. I'd stalled out in perhaps the most precarious position of the whole route. I considered grabbing the biner. With one pull, I'd be up and off.

Tourists' oblivious laughter spilled over the lip. Tons of people were up top. I was in a very private hell.

I stroked the biner a few times, fighting the urge to grab it but also thinking how foolish it would be to die on a slab, sliding and bouncing almost 2,000 feet to my death, when I could so easily save myself. My calves were slowly getting pumped. I knew I should do something soon, since treading water was only wearing me out. Downclimbing never occurred to me—I was going up (it was just a matter of how high) one way or another. But now, real fear seized me. Once again, I took a deep breath, studied the holds in front of me, and tried to think rationally about what I had to do.

Although I never wanted to be on that slab in the first place, I had to finish what I'd started without invalidating my ascent. Finally, I compromised. I kept my hand on the pathetic ripple but straightened my right index finger just enough for the tip of my last pad to rest on the bottom of the oval. My thought was, if my foot blew, I could snatch the biner with one finger and check my fall.

I smeared my foot, stood up, and grabbed the jug. No problem. I was delivered, free from my little prison, where I'd stood silently for a good five minutes. And I hadn't cheated by grabbing the biner.

I took the final 5.7 slab to the summit at a near run. Twenty or more hikers sat on the edge of the precipice, witnessing my final charge. But no one said a word. No yells, no pictures, nothing. Maybe they thought I was a lost hiker. Maybe they couldn't conceive of where I'd come from, or maybe they just didn't give a shit. When I mantled onto the actual top, I was met with a flood of humanity, a hundred-odd people spread across the summit plateau. Tourists ate lunch next to me. They made out, took scenic photos. People everywhere.

It was so weird. Like parachuting out of Vietnam into a shopping mall.

I was shirtless, pumped, panting. Psyched out of my mind. Flooded with conflicting emotions. I was embarrassed that I'd gotten scared on the slab. But I was thrilled beyond words to have finally done something that I'd been thinking about for months. Ashamed of myself for maybe pushing it a little further than I'd planned. Yet still proud of myself.

On the summit, part of me wished that someone, anyone, had noticed that I'd just done something noteworthy—though maybe it was better that I didn't have to talk to anybody. How could I have expressed what my last few hours had been like? It was enough that I knew.

I didn't make a sound. I took off my shoes and started hiking down the Cable route. It was only then that someone noticed. "Oh, my God," this dude blurted out. "You're hiking barefoot! You're so tough!"

D ESPITE ASCENDING AT A "SLOW JOG" rather than a "sprint," Alex completed the 2,000-foot climb, which spans twenty-three pitches for roped climbers, in the unthinkably short time of two hours and fifty minutes. Seven years later, no one else has seriously contemplated, let alone attempted, a free solo of the Regular Northwest Face on Half Dome.

Along with the outpouring of incredulous and wacky shout-outs on sites such as Supertopo.com, there was praise of the highest order from the peers who could best appreciate the magnitude of Alex's free solo. John Long, one of the original Stonemasters whom a younger Alex had regarded as a hero, commented, "There isn't anything else I can think of that requires that level of concentration, for that length of time, with the penalty being certain death if you make the tiniest mistake."

Sender Films got in touch with Alex, proposing to craft a twenty-two-minute film around reenactments of the Moonlight Buttress and Half Dome solos. *Alone on the Wall* would win prizes at mountain festivals all over North America and Europe, and turn Alex from a climbing prodigy into a minor celebrity.

None of this, however, went to Alex's head. "In the days after Half Dome," he reported, "any huge sense of gratification eluded me. I felt like I had kind of botched the climb. I'd gotten away with something. It wasn't a perfect performance."

In his climbing bible, he jotted his usual laconic entry to document the trailblazing free solo, downgrading the route even as he recorded it.

9-6-08

Reg NW Face—5.11d? <u>solo</u> 2:50 [2 hours 50 minutes] on route.
Higbee, 5.10 bypass. Sketchy on slab.

Alex closed the note with a sad-face emoticon, and the query to himself: "Do better?"

CHAPTER **THREE**

FEAR AND LOVING IN LAS VEGAS

A S ALEX BEGAN TO WIN a small measure of fame for his bold free solos, he started to taste the rewards of sponsorship. The first company to put him on board, through the championing of his climbing buddy Brad Barlage, was Black Diamond, the Utah-based firm that manufactures high-tech climbing gear as well as ski equipment and outdoor apparel. In the years to follow, Alex would win sponsorship from La Sportiva, Clif Bar, New England Ropes, and, most important, The North Face, whose "dream team" (officially known as the Global Team athletes) constitutes a roster of stellar rock climbers and mountaineers that is the envy of young aspirants worldwide. In 2014, the Ball Watch company, whose wristwatches fetch prices upwards of $2,500, ran full-page ads in the *New York Times Magazine* featuring a photo of Alex standing on Half Dome's Thank God Ledge, accompanied by the claim, "With no ropes and no protective gear, there is simply no room for error. That's why a dependable timepiece like Ball Watch is important in an environment with truly adverse conditions." Alex endorsed the product with the pithy phrase, "The watch that rocks," even though he never wears a watch of any kind on his wrist when he climbs.

In 2008, Boulder-based Sender Films, founded nine years earlier by Peter Mortimer as a bare-bones do-it-yourself video company, took notice of Alex. By then, Sender was putting out adventure films that were as well crafted and authentic as anything of their kind produced in this country or abroad. As Mortimer recalls, "We were hanging out in Yosemite a lot. Alex's solos of the Rostrum and Astroman were on our radar. We always have our ear to the ground, hoping to find the next hot young climber. Then when he soloed Moonlight Buttress, he really got our attention."

Mortimer adds, "Everybody else in our business was cranking out films about bouldering and sport climbing. I wasn't so interested in that. What I wanted to film was 'danger climbing'—big walls, big-range mountaineering on the cutting edge, and of course free soloing." For a new film titled *The Sharp End*, Mortimer and partner Nick Rosen enlisted a corps of strong young American rock climbers and set out for the Adršpach, a massif of steep sandstone towers just inside the Czech Republic near the German border, where it merges with the legendary Elbsandsteingebirge. (The "sharp end" is climbing jargon for going first on the rope, as the leader typically takes all the serious risks.)

The Sharp End is a glorious smorgasbord of wild exploits performed by adventurers in the United States and Europe. The episodes include trad "death routes" (extremely deficient in protection) in Eldorado Canyon near Boulder; long and sketchy aid climbing routes in Yosemite; alpine ventures on untouched spires in the Shafat Fortress of India; wingsuit BASE jumping off precipices in Switzerland; and free soloing, though the star in the film is not Alex but Steph Davis, who solves the 5.10+ Pervertical Sanctuary on the Diamond on Colorado's Longs Peak. Alex's role in the film is little more than a cameo appearance, but it dramatically foreshadows the stardom toward which he was headed. In fact, Sender chose for its movie jacket a still photo of Alex leading a desperate-looking pitch.

The Adršpach and Elbsandsteingebirge thrust out of the forest along the river Elbe, southeast of Dresden, in a wild burst of dark gray pinnacles. There, during the first two decades of the twentieth century, a cadre of hard men whose climbing culture was utterly insulated even from their peers in the Alps put up the most difficult rock routes anywhere in the world. As they did so, they developed a local style bound by ironclad "ethics" unlike that of any other scene.

Americans and Western Europeans discovered the Dresden arena only in the late 1960s, and when some of the best outsiders ventured there to sample that scene, they were uniformly impressed—and intimidated. By 2008, some forty years later, the purism of the eastern German and Czech locals still ruled the crags. In the Elbsandsteingebirge, big ring bolts, drilled frighteningly far apart (as much as twenty or thirty meters), form the only fixed anchors and protection. Pitons, nuts, and cams are not allowed. The only removable protection a climber is allowed to place is knotted nylon slings jammed into cracks—a practice with which American, French, and Swiss climbers were wholly unfamiliar. To make matters worse—or purer—chalk for the fingers is not allowed. Lacking decent rock shoes, the Dresden climbers put up many of their hardest routes barefoot.

Mortimer and Rosen rounded up their team of American rock stars, including Cedar Wright, Renan Ozturk, Matt Segal, Topher Donahue, and Heidi Wirtz. Alex went along as the promising rookie. For the film, the directors lured sixty-one-year-old Bernd Arnold— the grandmaster of the Elbsandsteingebirge from the late 1960s through the '70s and '80s—to act as guide for the awestruck Americans. In the film, although Arnold speaks virtually no English, he gleefully shows his charges the ropes (as it were), encouraging them to take off their shoes and scramble barefoot to get used to the strange rock. Arnold's comrades blithely underscore the seriousness of the routes with gallows humor. As one of them says, in accented English, "If you fall, you can become legend."

The climactic scene of this episode in *The Sharp End* unfolds after the Americans have succeeded on some of the classic routes but now want to make their own mark to salvage a bit of pride. They gather beneath a sharp vertical arête, a route that even the locals declare too dangerous. The talk is ominous and fearful. Wearing a hoodie, looking like the antisocial nerd Ben Smalley remembered from high school, Alex is almost silent. But then he quietly spouts, "We've been here for an hour, talking about how hard and how scary this is. We should just go do it."

So Alex takes the sharp end. His progress up the terrifying arête, superbly filmed, uses his buddies' spontaneous comments as voice-over. Cedar Wright says, "He's hesitating there for ten minutes. He's looking at a ninety-foot fall. He could hit the ground." In the film, you can hear Alex's short bursts of panting breath. But the smooth, exquisitely calculated movement is a work of art. Fear for his safety transmutes into his comrades' praise. "Watching Alex is pretty inspiring," one says, "because he keeps it together so well." Another: "Alex is in a different head space—his ability to stay calm and not get pumped, all the way to the top." And after Alex finishes the climb, yet another: "That's not a pitch I want to lead." Cedar Wright: "I'm definitely a little jealous."

Wordless, Alex stands on the summit of the spire and grins.

•   •   •   •

After Alex free soloed Half Dome in September 2008, Mortimer and Rosen decided they wanted to shape a whole film around the prodigy's extraordinary deeds. But no one had witnessed Alex's climbs on either Moonlight Buttress or Half Dome. The solution was self-evident: approach Alex and ask him whether he'd be willing to reenact passages on those two routes for the camera.

Mortimer remembers, "He wasn't reluctant at all. He was up for it. 'Yeah,' he told us, 'I love the idea of getting some footage on those walls.'"

The logistical problems of filming that footage, however, were monumental. By the spring of 2009, when Sender was ready to shoot Moonlight Buttress, there were several parties on the route, climbing it in old-fashioned style, with plenty of aid. Fortunately, those parties were toiling low on the route. Mortimer and still photographer Celin Serbo decided to rappel down some 400 feet from the summit, hang on parallel ropes, then film and photograph Alex free soloing the upper pitches close up with the aid parties well out of the frame. Alex would rappel down those 400 feet, take off his harness, and start soloing upward.

Mortimer had deep misgivings about what he was asking Alex to do. *What if he falls to his death,* he worried, *just for the sake of our film? I can't imagine how I could live with that.* His film crew was equally apprehensive. "As we gathered in Springdale the night before the reenactment," Mortimer says, "we were completely stressed out. We were at a pizza parlor. We waited until Alex went to the bathroom, then we said to each other, 'I don't know if we should do this.'

"When Alex came back, I started to ask, 'Alex, are you sure—?'

"He burst out, 'You guys are such pussies! You mean I'll have to call someone else to shoot this?'"

The passages Alex soloed for the camera were the 5.12 pitches above the crux 180-foot inside corner, where a perfect finger crack into which he locked his first digits had given him such exhilaration when he'd first soloed the route the previous April. Mortimer: "It was cold. And it was windy. The exposure up there at the top of Moonlight Buttress is crazy. It's as vertigo-inducing as anything on El Cap. While we filmed, just a few feet away from Alex, we were super careful not to move an inch, so as not to distract him. You don't want to drop a lens cap or knock loose even the tiniest stone."

Even so, Mortimer and his cameramen were gripped. The finger-locked digits, the feet pasted flat against the smooth wall, seemed to give Alex only the most marginal purchase on the world. Below him stretched an 800-foot void. If he fell, he might strike nothing before slamming into the ground at the base of the wall. At that moment, Alex turned to the camera and said, "So, do you want me to make this look like it's hard for me?" According to Mortimer, "Alex was actually thinking, 'Oh, those guys must be so bored.'" A little later, Alex jammed his knee into a crack, then suddenly let go with both hands. "No hands kneebar, baby!" he exulted.

A few months later, a slightly different crew, including Mortimer's directing partner Nick Rosen and cameraman Tim Kemple, gathered to shoot Alex reenacting parts of the Regular Northwest Face route on Half Dome. In the interim, two of America's best mountaineers, Johnny Copp and Micah Dash (both featured in *The Sharp End*, as they explored the Shafat Fortress in India and the Chamonix *aiguilles* in France), disappeared on Mount Edgar in western China, along with cinematographer Wade Johnson, who had worked on *The Sharp End*. Living in Boulder, all three were close friends of the entire staff of Sender Films. Not only that, but Sender was crafting a film around the attempt on the massive, unclimbed southeast face of Mount Edgar.

It was only when the trio missed a return flight out of Chengdu that a rescue effort was launched. Top climbers from Boulder and elsewhere, including Nick Rosen, immediately flew to China to initiate a search. They were aided by Chinese troops. On June 7, 2009, Copp's body was found at the base of the wall, Johnson's the next day. It seemed clear that a gigantic avalanche of mixed rock, snow, and ice had scoured the wall, engulfing the climbers. Dash's body was never found.

Remarkably, much of Johnson's footage was recovered intact at base camp. Mortimer and Rosen used it to put together a film in homage to their friends. *Point of No Return* is a haunting, unforgettable work. Knowing the tragic fate that awaits the three young climbers, you watch their tearful goodbyes to girlfriends at the airport, their boisterous antics at base camp, with a sense of mounting dread. But you also see the monstrously scary, nearly continuous barrage of falling rocks and ice that had made the trio decide to abandon the route even before coming to grips with it.

It's torturous to learn that the men's final mission was simply a scramble up to a cache above base camp to retrieve equipment they had stowed a few days before. Watching them head off to their doom, you want to scream at the screen, *Just go home! Leave the fucking gear!*

In the wake of the disaster, which shook the whole American climbing community, Mortimer and Rosen approached Half Dome with Alex in a somber, even psyched-out mood. "We had absolutely no stomach," says Mortimer, "for anything crazy or on the edge. We were going to restrict the filming to the easier pitches down low, then rap down a few hundred feet from the summit to film Alex finishing the Zig-Zags and traversing Thank God Ledge."

Despite the fears and sorrows of the filmmakers, *Alone on the Wall* comes across as a blithe celebration of climbing; it's even lighthearted in places. The film is a minor masterpiece. No one can watch it, even for the fourth or fifth time, without feeling palms turn sweaty as Alex performs his ropeless dance on vertical rock. And the film never fails to inspire a heated debate among climbers and nonclimbers alike over the ethics of free soloing. (Some nonclimbers simply cannot bear to watch the film.)

A testament to Mortimer and Rosen's cinematic skill lies in the fact that most viewers don't realize they're seeing a reenactment. Instead, the film looks and feels like a documentary of two of the boldest exploits of twenty-first-century climbing. For comic counterpoint, the film intercuts the footage on Moonlight Buttress and Half Dome with Alex giving a tour of the Econoline van that serves as his home (narrator Rosen: "Do you have girls in here a lot?" Alex, guffawing: "Do I look like I have girls in here a lot?"), and with a visit to Alex's childhood home in Sacramento, where his mother proudly shows off all the magazine covers featuring her son, while he cringes in embarrassment. The film closes lightheartedly, too, with Alex eating food out of a bowl with a twig in lieu of cutlery, as he riffs about being like a tool-using chimp using a stick to ferret out ants. "This is what makes us human," he cracks.

The heart of *Alone on the Wall*, of course, lies in the dazzling footage of Alex on his two big walls. Interspersed with this action are sound bites from Alex's peers. Says Cedar Wright, one of Alex's best friends, "When you meet Alex Honnold, you're gonna be like, 'Huh, this guy is a bumbling, dorky, awkward goofball.' Until he steps on the rock, and then he's literally a whole other person. He becomes this poised, graceful, calculated badass dude." John Long, the Stonemaster who shared in the first one-day ascent of the Nose on El Cap in 1975, marvels about Alex's free solo of Half Dome: "It took some vision to get up there, but it took some frickin' *balls* to actually do it." Climbing buddy Nick Martino declares, "Frickin' Honnold is walking on the moon, as far as I'm concerned."

As the footage of the actual climbing spools by, Alex comments in voice-over: "There's all the little things you have to think about, like left-right, which sequence you're doing, but there's nothing I'm really thinking about—I'm just doing it." And: "I love the simplicity of soloing. You never climb better than when you're soloing." And: "Doubt is the biggest danger in soloing. As soon as you hesitate, you're screwed." But even Alex seems at last to realize the magnitude of his deeds, as, standing on the summit of Moonlight Buttress, grinning with happiness, he utters, "When I think about it, it's frickin' rad!"

The climax of the film dramatizes the stall-out that gave Alex his five minutes of "very private hell" only 150 feet below the top of Half Dome. But Mortimer and Rosen were not about to ask Alex to repeat that terrifying sequence of "miserly smears" on the 5.12 slab above Thank God Ledge, where, on September 6, 2008, he had confronted the very real possibility of falling almost 2,000 feet to his death. Instead, in the film, Thank God Ledge itself serves as the locus for the freakout. As Alex sidles carefully away from the camera along the narrowing ledge, facing out with his back to the wall, he pauses. In voice-over, he narrates, "Basically, when I'm soloing, normally I have like a mental armor. You could say I'm in the zone. Something that's protecting my head from thinking too much. And for some reason"—he laughs at the memory—"on Half Dome I ran out of what armor I had. . . . I had a mini-nervous breakdown."

In the film, the invisible cameraman, Tim Kemple, tells Alex that he can traverse back to safety if he doesn't like the feel of this predicament. But Alex shuffles on—across ground that in reality was fairly easy for him. And then, soon, he's bounding across the summit, alone in his joy.

In only six years, that moment of film footage on Thank God Ledge became one of the most iconic images in climbing history. Sender Films put a still from the sequence on the cover of their boxed set *First Ascent*, which contains four other films besides *Alone on the Wall* and *Point of No Return*. A couple of years later, in its May 2011 issue, *National Geographic* ran a feature on the younger generation of Yosemite hotshots, for which photographer Jimmy Chin duplicated the shot. It made the cover of the magazine. In the 2014 Ball Watch ad, yet another version of Alex on Thank God Ledge illustrated the "truly adverse conditions" facing "the world's explorers."

Within the last year and a half, that image has spawned a craze of imitations, under the rubric "Honnolding," as climbers pose on their own ledges (much closer to the ground), their backs to the wall, feet together, arms stiff at their sides, blank looks on their faces—as well as a number of goofy parodies, in which subjects assume the same pose standing on toilet tanks, refrigerators, stepladders, and the like. The only comparable phenomenon in recent years was the vogue of Tebowing—kneeling in prayer, one knee on the ground, elbow on the other knee, closed hand pressed to bent forehead—in homage to the born-again NFL quarterback. After Tim Tebow moved off the field and on to ESPN, however, that craze waned fast.

Says Mortimer about the original photo of Alex on Thank God Ledge, "Something about that position brings home to everybody what the pros do on big walls, better than a conventional climbing shot does. It captures the vulnerability of it all. It's as if Alex is standing there, facing God. Completely vulnerable."

• • • •

Alone on the Wall promptly won grand prizes at film festivals ranging from Telluride, Colorado, to Trento, Italy, and Kendal, England. As perhaps the most dazzling presentation in the annual Reel Rock Tour, jointly sponsored by Sender Films and New York–based Big UP Productions, the film was screened in scores of venues all over the country in the fall of 2009. (By then, Reel Rock had already acquired a cult following.) More than the buzz about Alex's exploits humming on websites such as Supertopo.com, more even than a feature article in *Outside* magazine and the cover shot for *National Geographic*, the film put Alex on a map that covered far broader terrain than the insular world of hardcore climbing. (It's hard to think of a comparable case in the recent past of a young extreme athlete morphing from complete obscurity to considerable fame in only two years.) The film was the main impetus that convinced the CBS news program *60 Minutes* to film a profile of Alex, which aired on October 2, 2011. At the time of that widely watched TV segment, Alex was only twenty-six years old.

For several years, Alex had kept a Facebook page. Now, with this new explosion of media exposure, the page was inundated with shout-outs and queries from strangers. As Alex said in 2010, "I had to erase myself from Facebook. It was too crazy—I was getting twenty friend requests a day. Some kid would ask, 'Hey, what kind of chalk bag should I buy?' You hate to blow him off, but, like, what can you say?"

In September 2009, before Alex erased himself, a twenty-four-year-old woman attended the Reel Rock Tour at a Tucson screening. Stacey Pearson, who worked as nurse in a local hospital, was also a serious distance runner, having competed in four marathons, clocking a best time of three hours and twenty-five minutes.

As Pearson recalled in 2010, "I'd never heard of Alex Honnold. A friend invited me to Reel Rock, but I almost didn't go. We arrived late. Alex was just one of many characters in the films, but I thought, 'That guy is really cool.'

"I went home and Googled him. I discovered I could find him on Facebook. I wrote to him: 'I saw you on the film tour. I don't know anything about you, but I thought what you did was really respectful and cool.'"

Pearson got no answer for days, as Alex was in Siberia attending an international climbing meet. Eventually, however, he sent back a few words. "So I asked if I could friend him," said Pearson. "He accepted. He'd seen my picture and things about me, like my bio, where I called myself a 'future ultra-marathoner.' He wrote back, 'Are you really into ultra-marathoning?'

"We started e-mailing every few days," Pearson recalled. "Telling each other all about ourselves. Alex was in Spain, then he was in China, where they don't allow Facebook. So our e-mails grew longer and longer. Finally we did a video chat. It was nerve-racking. I was nervous, and I could tell he was, too. He had the hood on his sweat-shirt up. 'Hi,' he said. 'What's up?'"

At the time, Alex had no steady girlfriend. There had been

occasional brief liaisons, including a fling with Katie Brown, who a decade earlier had dazzled the climbing world as a teen prodigy, winning the world junior championship in Quebec at the age of fourteen. "Three weeks of wild torment," Alex later described his affair with Brown. "I was over-eager and under-suave."

"Alex was coming home on December 4, [2009]," Pearson recalled. "He mentioned that he was going to enter the California International Marathon in Sacramento two days later, to test his running capability. That seemed like a perfect excuse for us to meet at last, so I tried to sign up for the marathon, but unfortunately it was sold out. I decided to come to California anyway.

"I was a little nervous, but also excited—I was about to do something I'd never done before. I was waiting by the curb at the Oakland airport. Alex called to say he was fifteen minutes late. Finally he pulled up in his van. We may have hugged. It felt awkward. I was wearing a zebra print cardigan. Many months later, Alex told me that what I wore that day matched up to his standards of 'a hot girl'!

"It probably helped that our first time together was in the context of Alex's full-on family—his mom, Dierdre, and his sister, Stasia. It made things easier. The first night Alex gave a slide show for a small crowd at a pizza joint in Santa Rosa. I met a few of his friends. One of them said, 'Alex is a great guy.' I answered, 'Yeah, I've only known him for a day.'

"I waited at the halfway point of the marathon. When Alex came by, he gasped that he was starving. We ran together for a while. As we passed a guy carrying some food, Alex asked if he could have the banana in his hand, which the guy gladly handed over. Then we passed a small aid station with a few goodies. Alex's eyes grew wide when he spotted a bowl of M&M'S. He grabbed a handful and shoved them in his mouth. That's how I learned that his biggest weakness—so he says—is that he has an incurable sweet tooth."

Pearson returned to Tucson, and two weeks later Alex arrived for an extended visit. During their time together, they got to know each other. After Christmas, however, fed up with her job, Stacey took another gig as a nurse in Dallas. Thus began a two-year stint of working as a traveling nurse, changing jobs every few months as she rotated through hospitals all over the country.

Meanwhile, Alex was climbing in Yosemite. The pair spent a month and a half apart, before Alex came to Dallas for a second prolonged visit.

"I missed Alex," Stacey remembered, "even though I had no trouble making new friends in Dallas. When he visited, I made him do urban things, like going to museums and eating in good restaurants. We also ran and biked together. We fell in love for the first time in Dallas. But it's a big deal to say, 'I love you.' I made Alex say it first."

Twenty-nine years old in 2015, Stacey is a very pretty woman with light brown hair, striking gray-blue eyes, and an infectious smile. Slender and extremely fit, she comes across at first as quiet and sweet-tempered, but on further acquaintance, she reveals a sharp intelligence and a stubborn will that are a match for Alex's.

In early 2010, even as they fell in love, certain conflicts and incompatibilities emerged. "I felt uncomfortable sleeping in his van," Stacey recalled. "I had trouble adjusting to it. I felt dirty, gross, and cramped." The two argued about lifestyle. Stacey drinks moderately, Alex not at all. She enjoyed a regular social life with friends, but Alex still felt ill at ease in such situations. In turn, Alex thought of Stacey as insufficiently outdoorsy, and he worried that her commitment to nursing might not blend with his nomadic lifestyle. A joking to-and-fro that had begun in their e-mails became a teasing conversational routine. Hanging over it all was the possibility that, as so many of his friends feared, Alex might kill himself free soloing.

According to Stacey, "I would say, 'If you die one day, I can fly to Europe and find my dream European guy.' He would fire back, 'If you're hit by a bus, I can go hang out with the French chicks.'"

During the next five years, Stacey and Alex remained a couple. They discussed marriage and kids but committed to neither. Along the way, they had their share of fallings-out, and even several break-ups that both thought were likely to be terminal.

The first bad patch came in April 2010, toward the end of what Stacey would later look back on as a three-month "honeymoon period" after they'd finally met in Sacramento the previous December.

Stacey was in Dallas, but her nursing contract had been terminated early, so she was planning to move to Los Angeles. We hadn't actually broken up, but I suspected she was getting into this other dude in Dallas. In Yosemite, I'd been hoping to climb something rad, but the weather was shitty, raining every day, everything wet. Meanwhile, I knew the weather was perfect in Las Vegas. So I thought I could try my luck at Red Rocks, the great massif of sandstone cliffs just a few miles west of the city.

Stacey and I had made vague plans to meet in Tucson, as she drove from Dallas to L.A. So for me, heading down to Vegas was a kind of move toward our rendezvous in Tucson and, I hoped, toward saving our relationship.

Because of the weather, I hadn't been able to climb anything super-exciting in the Valley, so I'd done nothing but boulder. And if you boulder too much, the skin on your fingers gets raw and tender—worthless for sustained climbing. So I was in an angst-driven mood anyway, on top of the angst about Stacey.

I grew up reading climbing stories by Mark Twight, aka Doctor Doom. He was famous for dwelling on pain and heartbreak and existential suffering as the spurs that drove him to tackle more and more out-there routes. It's not that he was suicidal—in fact, he called climbing "a tool to forestall suicide." A whole generation of young climbers, myself included, was inspired by the essays in his collection, Kiss or Kill: Confessions of a Serial Climber. (If I reread it today, I suspect I'd see the affectation behind the carefully con-. structed persona of Doctor Doom.) But Twight also wrote Extreme Alpinism, the manifesto that pretty much defined the new style of light, fast, go-for-broke ascents.

Still, there's a rich vein in mountaineering literature of climbers using dark thoughts and stormy moods to precipitate cutting-edge climbs, especially solos. Angst as a motivator. I think an old issue of Climbing magazine ran a long piece detailing how romantic breakups had prompted rad solo climbs. Nerve-racking tales about emotionally wrecked men risking it all in an effort to sort out their feelings.

It's not necessarily suicidal. It's about a guy suddenly losing the love of his life, caring a little less about danger, and so finally doing something that he's always kept tucked in the back of his mind.

I've never felt suicidal myself. But trying to save my relationship with Stacey that April was stressing me out. I was definitely in a dark spell in my life.

Anyway, at first I envisioned a quick stop at Red Rocks for some mellow soloing in dry, warm conditions, then on to Tucson for the mission that was the real point of my trip. But I was also thinking about a great classic line, the Original Route on Rainbow Wall. In fact, it's been called the finest of all the thousands of routes at Red Rocks. At the head of Juniper Canyon, the Original Route is fourteen pitches of sustained climbing up this massive, concave, amphitheaterlike face, lots of it on tiny holds, up to 5.12b in difficulty. And the crux comes high, on the tenth pitch.

The route was first climbed in 1973 with a fair amount of aid, and rated at 5.9 A2. (Traditional aid grades in the YDS system range from A0—easiest—to A5.) The first free ascent came in 1997 by Leo Henson and Dan McQuade. I'd onsighted the route three or four years before with Josh McCoy, but that was my only previous trip up the route, and I certainly didn't have the moves dialed.

On the way to Vegas, I called up all the friends I could think of to ask if any of them wanted to do the Rainbow Wall. Nada. They were all busy with something or other. In my angst-driven mood, I made a snap decision: Fuck it, I'll do it anyway.

All the way on the road from Yosemite across Nevada, I was preoccupied with thoughts about Stacey. But ever since I'd first seen the route, even before I climbed it, Rainbow Wall had been embedded in my consciousness. I'd dreamed for years about free soloing the Original Route.

So, on April 28, I found myself at the Pine Creek parking lot, the wall looming above me. My mind was jangling with a dozen interwoven streams of thought. The wind was blowing at close to gale force, and while that didn't help my confidence, a rational part of my mind was grateful that my skin would stay dry and cool on the wall. Then, with perfect timing, Stacey called me on my cell phone. We had a very pleasant, if brief conversation. She tentatively reconfirmed our plan to meet in Tucson. Suddenly the desert morning seemed rosier, and I almost thought I could see a rainbow.

Even at the time, I knew that it probably wasn't healthy to feel such euphoria over a girl. But I embraced the mood and harnessed it to my purpose, starting my hiking with determination and glee. Alone in the canyon, I listened to the various bird calls and the sound of water babbling through the boulder-strewn wash. Suddenly all those little things seemed so much more meaningful, and I was overcome with gratitude that I could be having such a great time in such a beautiful place.

I suppose I should have realized that I was becoming emotionally unhinged. But I wanted to maintain my elation as long as I could, maybe even to the top of the route. I focused on how exciting the climbing would be, how much I craved the challenge, how beautiful the whole region was. Behind all that sensory delight floated the real excitement, which was that maybe, just maybe, Stacey did actually care for me, and we might be able to make things work. My mind was layered like an onion, though I suppose at the core lay the deep sadness that things might be ending.

But I made it all the way to the base of the wall in my semi-blissful state, and once there my mind turned practical. Finally I could stop trying to control my mood and focus solely on the climbing. I knew that this would be where I really found peace, in the intricacies of 11+ stem corners and 12a liebacking. As usual, it took me a few pitches to find my groove, but once I got moving I really did feel peaceful. I flowed up pitch after pitch of perfect corners. The amazing flat edges that appeared from time to time were a delight to use, and I found my position on the cliff stunning.

Free soloing this route after only one previous roped ascent of it—and that several years earlier—amounted to the polar opposite of the kind of superpreparation I had applied to Moonlight Buttress a little more than a year before. In some sense, I had no idea what I was doing up there on Rainbow Wall. Some people might call this crazy. I prefer to think of it as badass. It definitely amped up the adventure. This time, it felt like I was onsighting again—only without a rope. I remembered the odd move here and there, but most of it felt like I was discovering the sequences for the first time. There's no question, though, that my impulsive push on Rainbow Wall had everything to do with what was going on with Stacey.

About halfway up the route, there's a stretch of easy pitches, ranging from 5.4 to 5.8, that wanders up and to the right through ramps to a cozy perch on Over the Rainbow Ledge. Here, my mind turned back to "real" life, with all the angst I had carried with me from the Valley, but fortunately, that "down" interlude was fleeting. Soon enough, I was facing the crux tenth pitch.

I was about 750 feet off the ground. I was palming and stemming up this corner on really small ripples in the sandstone. All of a sudden, I realized what the crux required. You'd have to get your feet as high as you could, then jump to grab a jug. A true "dyno" move, but not such a big deal if you were roped and had placed some solid pro nearby. Maybe that's why I didn't remember it from my previous ascent. But now I got there, looked at the jug out of reach, imagined jumping for it, and said to myself, Hell, no!

I could still have downclimbed to Over the Rainbow Ledge, traversed right, and finished the wall by the indirect Swainbow variation, which is only 5.10. But in the mood I was in, I wanted to finish what I'd set out to do. Four or five times I climbed up those ripples, surveyed the situation, and climbed back down. It was simply out of the question to jump for the jug. If you don't catch the hold, you're off and down . . . and dead.

Slowly an alternative dawned on me. Just in reach from the ripples was a tiny divot, a natural hole in the stone caused by a black iron-oxide intrusion. I could sink only about a third of the first digit of my left index finger into the divot, then stack my middle finger and my thumb on top of it. It would be the ultimate crimp, and I'm sure the divot had never been used before. Finally, I committed my whole weight to the jammed tip of my finger, smeared an opposing foot against the corner, and pulled. My finger in the divot held, and I grabbed the jug with my other hand. Strangely, instead of fear, I felt complete serenity as I made the move.

The next pitch was a 5.12 lieback. I thought it would be a lot easier than the pitch before, but it was pretty gnarly in its own right. Wait, I thought, this shouldn't be so hard. And now I had no option of downclimbing, because there was no way I would ever reverse that crimp on the divot. But I kept it together and finished the lieback.

The last two pitches flew by in a blur. I finally felt completely warmed up and climbed with ease. But as soon as I topped out on the summit, the driving wind nearly knocked me over. On the wall, I'd been protected from the gusts, but here I was fully exposed to the brunt of the gale. When you're free soloing, of course, rappelling the route isn't an option, since you don't have a rope. Now I cowered in a little hole and changed out of my rock shoes into approach shoes that I'd carried in a small backpack, along with a little food and water.

The descents from Moonlight Buttress and Half Dome had been pretty routine, down trails that scores of hikers trod every day, and it wasn't a strain to go down barefoot. The descent from Rainbow Wall, on the other hand, was heinous. It's a series of technical scrambles on slick sandstone slabs, all the way back to the limestone mountains west of Red Rocks, to gain the upper drainage of Oak Creek Canyon. Then all the way down Oak Creek as you circle the peak of which Rainbow Wall is the northeast face. The whole descent is a bit of a bear, really heavy on the scrambling.

Then, hiking the flat desert back to my van, I felt like I was on a death march—no food or water. Just endless walking.

And now, in an instant, the sense of peace that had carried me up the climb vanished. Away from the tranquillity of the wall, my psyche started to fray. I was exultant at having soloed the wall but suddenly much less optimistic about my "real" life. As I thrashed my way down, I wondered if I really would be able to salvage my relationship with Stacey, and whether or not it was even worth the effort. As the canyon drew out in front of me and the afternoon heat bore down harder on me, the world seemed so much less beautiful than it had on the hike in. By the time I'd reached the flat desert and started circling back toward my van, I was much less pleased with my performance and fairly sure I would soon be single. My mind sank as low as it had gone high, and I seemed powerless to keep it under control. The whole experience had left me a little raw. The constant howl of wind, the crushing heat of the sun, hunger, thirst, mental fatigue—they all left me feeling vulnerable.

As soon as I reached the van, my first thought was to check my phone to see if Stacey had called. I think we'd made some vague agreement to chat later. I hoped she had left a message. But I knew that she hadn't. Unsurprisingly, no call, which I took to mean that Stacey just wasn't very psyched about "us."

The sandwiches I made helped ease my disappointment. I planned on soloing another route in the afternoon, just so I could finish all my business at Red Rocks in one day and keep on driving toward my real goal—Tucson.

• • • •

I was pleased with myself for soloing the Rainbow Wall. Maybe I should have called it a day, but I'd already decided I wanted to do more. My plan was to solo up Prince of Darkness, a seven-pitch 5.10 route that soars through a blank-looking face on Black Velvet Wall. Then I'd downclimb another 5.10 route, Dream of Wild Turkeys, which joins Prince of Darkness about 650 feet off the ground.

I chatted with some other climbers in the parking lot, joking about the terrible weather in Yosemite, then drove over to the trail-head for Black Velvet Canyon. But now the euphoria was long gone, replaced by lethargy and the deep fatigue of my worn-out mind. I'd always thought that Prince of Darkness would be a good challenge for me in dealing with the exposure of tiny holds on a smooth vertical wall. I never considered calling it quits, but on the way to the base I found that I didn't really care. I was sick of the unrelenting wind and my feet hurt from hiking and edging. The wall didn't excite me.

Since I was already warmed up and in a soloing mindset, I

expected the climbing to be smooth and effortless. But instead I felt jerky and slow. I wasted energy by overgripping the sandstone crimps and worrying about breaking footholds. I didn't want to be there. Instead of relishing the process, the whole experience of being on the wall, I just wanted to have it finished. I wanted to be back in my van, out of the wind.

I kept trudging upward, though I never got comfortable. My feet hurt more and more, but I never passed a good-enough stance to adjust my shoes. By the time I reached the top of the route— the large ledge where Prince of Darkness joins Dream of Wild Turkeys—I hated climbing, hated the wind, and wanted to go home. On the ledge, I took off my shoes for a while, trying to allow some blood to flow back into my toes. I didn't look around the canyon, I didn't admire the shadows lengthening across the desert, I just looked at my feet and waited to start the descent.

I downclimbed Dream of Wild Turkeys, which turned out to be a pretty fun route. Or at least it would have been fun in a different time and place. As I descended, I would occasionally find myself having a good time. And then suddenly the wind would pick up and I would realize that I had only been enjoying a brief reprieve. But I suppose that the wind and my fatigue combined to blunt all my other emotions. I just didn't care as much. Everything to do with "real" life, including Stacey, seemed a little less critical. What really mattered was sitting down in a sheltered place and eating. And maybe sleeping.

• • • •

That evening, I met some friends for dinner in Las Vegas. In the bathroom of the restaurant, I washed my hands for the first time and discovered I had a blood blister on my left index finger, where I'd jammed it into the iron-oxide divot, stacked a finger and a thumb on top of it, and made that pioneering move up to grab the jug. I came back to the table and showed the blistered fingertip to my friends. It felt like a badge of courage.

That marathon day of veering emotions at Red Rocks was like a whole life in a nutshell. As it turned out, though, I didn't wait for the rendezvous in Tucson. The next day I flew to Dallas, ostensibly to help Stacey pack for her move to L.A. But I really wanted to win her back. I basically re-wooed her. And it worked . . . for a while.

Two months later, we broke up—for the first time.

CHAPTER **FOUR**
WORLD TRAVELER

ALEX HAD PULLED OFF his three-route tour de force at Red Rocks in the same purist, private style that he had wielded on Moonlight Buttress and Half Dome. No one had witnessed his climbing on Rainbow Wall, Prince of Darkness, or Dream of Wild Turkeys, and only the folks with whom he had chatted at the trailhead around midday had any idea that he was up to anything special. But the word got out quickly. On Supertopo.com, veteran Yosemite climber Peter Haan—who in the early 1970s had dazzled his peers with first free ascents and roped solos of classic routes (using a complicated self-belaying system)—reported Alex's Red Rocks feat on May 12, 2010, only fourteen days after Alex had battled his demons in gale-force winds on those sandstone walls.

The response was another medley of disbelief, astonishment, congratulations, and cautionary screeds begging Alex not to risk his life so cavalierly. "You messing with us, Peter?" wrote another Valley veteran, invoking the kind of incredulity that had led some to dismiss Moonlight Buttress as an April Fools' Day hoax. But a believer posted, "This fella should try walking on water." Another veteran weighed in: "Having done all 3 routes, this just makes me sick."

Many of the responders expressed simple admiration. "Long live Alex Honnold," cheered one. "Another amazing send by a super nice dude!" John Long, the Stonemaster who would bear on-screen witness to Alex's genius in *Alone on the Wall*, posted simply, "Alexander the Great."

The cautionary comments, however, verged on the avuncular. "I hope Alex is being careful, he's such a great kid," one observer ventured. "It seems that Alex has taken it to a new level only by cutting the safety margin drastically. I'd feel more comfortable if his solos were cracks [as opposed to small holds on otherwise blank walls]. One thing is for sure, he has courage beyond belief."

So far in his career, the climbs that have won Alex the greatest acclaim have come in even-numbered years. Moonlight Buttress and Half Dome in 2008, Rainbow Wall in 2010, then other incredible breakthroughs in 2012 and 2014. Alex is aware of this pattern, referring to the odd-numbered years as periods of "consolidation." But in some sense, this schema belies the nonstop virtuosity of Alex's approach to climbing in all its forms.

In April 2009, for instance, Alex joined a team headed for Mount Kinabalu, at 13,435 feet the highest peak in Borneo. By its easiest route, Kinabalu is a tourist-thronged walk-up, but the mountain is actually a gigantic monolith of granite soaring out of dense rain forest. Some of its earliest explorers got lost in the jungle just trying to find their way to the mountain, and even today, Kinabalu still has untouched walls that challenge the best mountaineers.

The trip was the brainchild of Mark Synnott. Thirty-nine years old at the time, Synnott was a veteran mountaineer with a record of bold first ascents all over the globe. By 2009, he had perfected the art of getting magazine assignments combined with corporate sponsorship (usually by The North Face) to launch exotic adventures in the far corners of the world, his teams comprising some of the top American climbing stars. For *Men's Journal* and Borneo, he recruited Conrad Anker (who found George Mallory's body on Everest in 1999), photographer Jimmy Chin, filmmaker Renan Ozturk, and Kevin Thaw—all four veterans of other landmark expeditions. Anker, who had become the team captain for The North Face, had recently anointed the wunderkind of Moonlight Buttress and Half Dome with TNF sponsorship.

Now Anker tried to convince Synnott to add the twenty-three-year-old Honnold to the Borneo team. Says Synnott now, "I was pretty apprehensive. I'd never met Alex. In general, I don't like going off with guys I don't already know. There's a big potential for personality conflicts. And Alex had never been on an expedition."

The team's objective was an unclimbed, nearly vertical wall on the north side of the mountain, rising out of a forbidding abyss called Low's Gully. The place had an evil reputation, cemented by a catastrophe in 1994 when a ten-man British army team out on what was supposed to be a six-day training mission got entangled in a thirty-one-day survival ordeal. That disaster was vividly recounted in the book *Descent into Chaos*, by journalist Richard Connaughton.

Synnott had another source for his misgivings. Aware of Alex's deeds as a free soloist, Synnott worried "what kind of insane stuff" the young hotshot "might pressure me into doing." As it turned out, the two got along well in Borneo. "We hit it off right off the bat," Synnott remembers. "Alex has a wide-open personality. He deals with people well. There's no pretense. No bullshit."

Still, there were "quirky little things" that caused minor disputes between the leader and the rookie. "On his rack," Synnott claims, "he set up all his cams the way he would in Indian Creek"—the crag in southern Utah famed for short, steep crack climbs. This meant that Alex couldn't free up carabiners to use in all the different ways mountaineering requires. "So I had to take his rack apart," Synnott adds.

"'What are you doing?' Alex asked me.

"'Dude, this doesn't work here.'"

According to Synnott, Alex "wouldn't use shoulder slings"—long nylon loops that minimize drag by redirecting the climbing rope as it zigzags from one piece of protection to the next.

"What do you do about rope drag?" Synnott asked him.

"I just skip pieces," Alex answered. (In other words, he runs out his lead much farther than normal between points of pro, risking much longer leader falls.)

"Alex didn't like to use little stoppers" (the smaller styles of nuts for protection). "He said, 'I don't need this shit.' Then he'd get to a place where there were only tiny cracks, and he'd say, 'Wow, nothing else fits.'

"Alex had been living in this Yosemite bubble, where you don't need to learn all the tricks of mountaineering."

Despite those quirks, on Kinabalu, Synnott admits admiringly, "Alex did some pretty sick stuff"—long, highly technical leads with a minimum of protection.

The deft, amusing piece that Synnott wrote for the March 2010 issue of *Men's Journal* opens with a scene at the base of the wall in which a priceless bit of repartee evokes the "Yosemite bubble."

"Where's your helmet?"

"Uh, I don't have one," Alex replies, looking me square in the eyes and without apology.

"What do you mean? You forgot it back in camp?"

Before I finish my question, I know the answer.

"Uh, no. I mean I didn't bring one on the trip."

"Intentionally?"

"Sort of."

But when Alex leads the terrifying, almost unprotected crux pitch of the long climb, before the two men settle in to bivouac on a suspended platform called a portaledge, Synnott hails the prodigy's accomplishment.

Two hours later he reached the shelter of a small roof, 150 feet above me. It was, hands down, one of the best leads I'd ever witnessed. . . .

[Conrad] Anker was right. I was learning things from Honnold. . . . He brought something to the expedition none of us anticipated. Every jaw-dropping lunge, every inhuman pull, even every rookie mistake—it all rekindled the fire that we had back when we were his age. And it showed me, at least, that the fire was still there. Later, as we settled into our sleeping bags in the porta-ledge, Honnold needed to get something off his chest. "You know, I'm kind of feeling like a pansy," he confessed. "How so?" I replied. "You just did the sickest lead I've ever seen." "I know," he replied, "but it scared me. I shouldn't have gotten so scared."

Conrad Anker was one of *my first mentors. I'd always admired the guy, not only for his great climbs such as the Shark's Fin on Meru Peak in the Garhwal Himalaya and his first ascents with Alex Lowe of wild-looking towers in Queen Maud Land in Antarctica, but also because of the way he lives his life. Conrad calls himself a Buddhist, and he constantly preaches and practices kindness to others and doing good for the planet. The school in the Khumbu Valley he started years ago to train Sherpas in technical climbing is a prime example of Conrad's altruistic service to others. And it was Conrad who convinced The North Face to spon-*

sor me, which really improved my climbing opportunities. So even though I knew almost nothing about Borneo, I was psyched to be invited by Mark Synnott to go along on the Kinabalu expedition.

All six of us got along well during that trip, and it's true that Mark and I hit it off from the start. But it was a really long expedition—a full month from April 2 to May 1, 2009. I was used to getting things done a lot faster—one-day ascents of big walls in the Valley, for instance. There were times during the trip when our sluggish progress nearly drove me crazy. After five days in Low's Gully, we'd gotten nowhere on the wall. I kept saying to myself, Why is this taking so long?

The "quirky little things" that got between Mark and me had as much to do with our difference in age as with our climbing styles. Like when Mark tried to take apart my rack—that just sent me off the deep end. I liked to think I knew how to handle my own cams and biners.

As for skipping pieces rather than building up rope drag, I do that all the time. It just depends on whether the terrain is danger-ous or not. And Mark's I-told-you-so about the stoppers isn't the way I remember it. On the whole route, I doubt that I placed a single nut, because the wall was one pitch after another of over-hanging granite. He was just too old-school for my taste.

For instance, Mark led one pitch of pure choss—crumbly rock, loose holds everywhere. It was about 5.7, but Mark aided it. He even drilled a bolt. He took forever to lead the pitch. I said to him, "Dude, it's just five-seven. Why don't you just climb it? It's not really dangerous if you tread lightly." But he was going, "Oh, man, this is really sketchy!" Once he got his anchor in, I toproped the pitch in about three and a half minutes.

Mark later took me to task for an awkward moment when he wanted Jimmy Chin to shoot some film in which I would talk about what it was like to have Conrad as a mentor. I balked. Mark thought this meant that I wasn't open to being taught by my team-mates. But back then, it was a lot harder for me to perform in front of the camera, especially with all the guys standing around, including Conrad. It felt like, "Okay, Alex, talk about this. Dance, monkey!" So I'd have to start dancing.

There was a slightly weird dynamic going on among us as a team. I knew going into the trip that none of the other guys was as good a rock climber as I was. But they were all badass moun-taineers, and I figured I'd be learning a bunch of stuff from them. Halfway through, though, I just felt, This isn't the way we should be doing this climb.

The big problem on Kinabalu is rain. We'd been climbing low on the wall for about a week before we committed to the full thrust, leaving our base camp behind. On only the second day on that push, a huge squall came over the mountain from the north. Mark and I settled in to the portaledge, while Conrad tried to push the route above. In his Men's Journal article, Mark played this up as do-or-die drama—which is what the magazines want:

> Massive waterfalls were now pouring off the cliff, and the gully below started to roar as it transformed into a raging rapid. Even if we had wanted to bail, there was no way out but up. Above, I could hear muffled yelling, followed by an alarming amount of rockfall. Anker was somewhere above us doing battle in the chaos.

The truth of the matter, though, was that the Kinabalu climb just wasn't that rad. I felt that we could always have rapped off the route if we had to, and by 2009, Low's Gully didn't figure anymore as the hellish abyss that had trapped the British army guys fifteen years earlier. Still, we spent twenty-four hours on the portaledge getting soaked. Since Jimmy Chin and Mark took up all the space on the portaledge, as the rookie I got the shitty seat. I had to sling a hammock beneath the portaledge, suspended from its corners, which made for a very awkward body position. The water dripped through the floor of the portaledge onto my hammock and sleeping bag. I sort of sat in a puddle for a whole day and night. It was all right as long as I didn't move and stir up the water. I was reading The Brothers Karamazov, which fit the dreary mood. I tore the paperback in half and gave Mark the first part to read. Pretty grim, but I guess it builds character.

The weather cleared off enough so that we could finish the climb the next day. The last pitches were actually easy. After a brief celebration on the summit, we rapped the whole wall with our bags and hauled them back out the other side of Low's Gully. It was an ordeal. I think the reason we did this is because we didn't want to haul everything to the top of the wall. We just left it all in the middle and then lowered it to the ground in one huge lower.

In the Men's Journal article, Mark wrote some really nice things about me, even if they were still tinged with paternalism.

> Sharing a rope with Honnold had made me think a lot about what I was like when I was his age, and I couldn't help but draw comparisons to myself. I was never close to as talented as he is, nor was I as bold, but I did have a youthful hunger and my tolerance for risk was more than a little excessive. Honnold reminded me that climbing without risk isn't really climbing at all.

And he ended the piece with this summit vignette:

> Looking over at Honnold, I couldn't help but wonder if he understood the arc that we all seem to follow as climbers any better after hanging out with a bunch of old-timers, if he understood that he would have to ultimately accept the fact that if you're going to climb as hard as he does now his whole life, and live to tell the tales,

he was going to need a little bit of luck. These days I've got kids waiting for me to return from expeditions like these, and there's a line I just don't cross anymore. The problem is figuring out where that line is at any given moment. Honnold is one of the brightest and most talented climbers I've ever met. If nothing else, I think he knows that climbing is the kind of sport that will sort you out, one way or another.

After the expedition was over, for all my impatience with the old-school style the other guys seemed to think the route required, I realized that I owed a lot to Mark. He was probably right about my "Yosemite bubble." In Borneo, I realized that climbing in remote ranges did entail all kinds of techniques I hadn't had to learn on Half Dome or El Cap.

Mark had truly broadened my climbing experience. His whole thing—exploring, traveling the world, having adventures in exotic places—was new to me, and exciting.

Because, when all was said and done, we'd forged a good friendship. Mark invited me on his next media- and sponsor-supported junket, a truly exploratory climbing trip to an untouched desert landscape full of weird pinnacles and arches in northeastern Chad, in Africa. The trip was planned for November 2010. Without a moment's hesitation, I signed on.

• • • •

Mark had discovered the Ennedi Desert by staring hard at satellite photos. On a previous expedition to Cameroon, he started wondering about the climbing possibilities in Chad, which borders Cameroon on the northeast. Civil war in the Sudan had provoked a refugee crisis in Chad, making it an inhospitable country for Westerners to visit, but Mark loves that sort of challenge. He knew that expeditions had been active in the Tibesti Mountains, near the northern border of Chad, but the much more remote Ennedi seemed untouched by climbers. And the satellite photos made it clear that the rock formations there were spectacular.

For his team, Mark put together two threesomes. What he called his "media team," whose main mission was to film and photograph (even though all three were good climbers), consisted of Jimmy Chin, Renan Ozturk, and Tim Kemple. The "climbing team" was Mark, James Pearson, and myself. James is a Brit who'd made quite a splash on the gritstone crags of his native country, then had taken his act abroad. He was about the same age as me. I'd climbed with James for a day or two in the U.K., but I didn't really know him. I sensed, though, that his outlook on climbing matched mine a lot better than the more old-school mountaineers I'd gone to Borneo with. By 2010, like me, he was sponsored by The North Face.

Sparsely inhabited today, the Ennedi had once been a thriving homeland to seminomadic pastoralists who herded everything from goats and cattle to camels. The vivid rock art of the region—pictographs painted in red, white, brown, and black—was first discovered in the 1930s. The human figures abound in archers leaping and dancing as they carry their bows. By now, archaeologists have been able to use the rock art to date and define a series of cultures ranging back all the way to 5000 BC.

We arrived in N'Djamena, Chad's capital, in mid-November. One thing Mark is really good at is arranging logistics in developing countries. For our excursion, he'd recruited an Italian expat named Piero Rava, who at the age of sixty-six ran a trekking company taking foreigners on ambitious photo tours of places like the Ennedi. Piero was a veteran mountaineer himself, having participated in a bold Italian expedition to Cerro Torre in Patagonia in 1970. An amazing spire of granite and ice, Cerro Torre had once earned the reputation as "the world's most difficult mountain." Another Italian, Cesare Maestri, claimed to have reached the summit in 1959, only to have his partner, the Austrian Toni Egger, die on the descent when he was avalanched off the wall. Other climbers doubted the ascent, and it is now generally regarded as a complete hoax, with Maestri and Egger getting nowhere near the top.

The Italian team in 1970 got to within 200 meters of the summit. Had they succeeded, they would have claimed the true first ascent, which was finally pulled off four years later by a team led by Casimiro Ferrari, who had been Piero's teammate in 1970. It was cool to have a Cerro Torre veteran leading our expedition, and even cooler to know that Piero had fifteen years' experience in taking trekkers to the Ennedi. He had checked out lines on the arches and pinnacles, but he hadn't climbed anything, and he assured us that no other climbers had touched the rock there.

Piero spoke almost no English but good French. So I ended up translating for the crew in the jeep. The whole process was kind of fun.

Borneo had been my first taste of a true Third World adventure, but Chad was far more intense. And the impact on me of those three weeks in Africa would be life-changing, in ways I never could have foreseen.

We set off from N'Djamena in a Land Rover and a pair of Toyota Land Cruisers. The Ennedi was 625 miles away as the crow flies, but a lot farther as we ended up traveling. In an essay about the trip, Mark later captured the surreal flavor of our drive:

We had been traveling Chad's only paved road for less than an hour when Piero suddenly veered off into the sand. I assumed we were stopping, but Piero just pointed the vehicle northeast and kept going—for the next four days.

Sometimes we followed rutted tracks in the sand, while other times it seemed like we were driving across areas that had never

*seen a vehicle. In the softer sand, the only way we could maintain
headway was to drive at 60 mph, with the vehicle skimming pre-
cariously at the limit of control. When we stopped to camp at night,
our Chadian mechanic would work on the vehicles, cleaning out air
filters and sometimes replacing or repairing various engine parts.*

*We put in long, grueling days of four-wheeling, sometimes going
from sunup to sundown seeing nothing but flat sand. The key was
to spend as much time as possible in Piero's lead vehicle, because
in the following vehicles you lived in a cloud of dust, which worked
its way into every orifice of your body. It was the beginning of the
Chadian winter, and the temperature hovered in the 90s during the
day. In summer, Piero explained, it got up to 140°F.*

The other guys tended to space out or try to sleep during this
endless, monotonous journey, but I was transfixed. With my face
glued to the window, I stared out at the emptiness, watching for any
change in the horizon. On our second day in the sand, we had an
encounter that turned into a minor epiphany for me.

Suddenly I saw two men riding camels in the desert ahead
of us. Piero slowed down for them and stopped a short distance
away. In retrospect, I wonder if he was stopping only because he
was used to his tourists wanting to take pictures of such things,
or if he was truly stopping out of courtesy to interact with them,
the way hikers do when they're out in the backcountry. Regard-
less, we piled out of the jeeps and approached the nomads, one
of whom dismounted and poured us a large bowl of camel milk.
Piero explained that nomads will always offer you something as
hospitality, even though they don't have much for themselves. We
declined his offer, taking a few pictures instead. Piero gave the
two men the leftovers from our breakfast, explaining to us that it
was normal for them to travel for days without any real food. They
mounted their camels and continued into the desert.

Later I asked Piero how those nomads could navigate so accurately in the desert, especially when the stakes were so high. A slight mistake in bearing would mean missing the next well and dying of dehydration in the middle of nowhere. Piero explained that they use the sun and the direction of the wind, which is constant in the winter, to navigate. When I protested that it seemed like too serious a situation to rely only on the sun and wind, Piero drew an analogy to climbing. Sometimes you find yourself in positions where falling would mean death. So you don't fall. It helped me understand. The nomads just don't make mistakes.

Occasionally, when we passed a small oasis, we'd run into native people, small clusters of men, women, and children living in mud huts or thatched dwellings. These were Toubous, so unused to seeing strangers—especially white-skinned Westerners—that Piero warned us not to approach them or take photographs of them.

Still, I stared in fascination at these seminomadic desert dwellers. And here I had another, more lasting epiphany. After the trip was over, it wasn't the climbing that stuck foremost in my memory. It was the days of driving across the desert to and from the Ennedi. My lasting impressions were of kids beating donkeys to make them haul water faster, or of men riding camels through the middle of nowhere, or of other men working all day to turn mud into bricks. I was seeing a completely different way of life from any I'd ever witnessed before, in a completely alien place. The simple facts of Chadian life—what it takes to survive in that kind of climate with nothing but a hut and some animals—stunned me.

And this made me realize, perhaps for the first time, how easy my life was compared to those of people in less privileged societies. That insight would lead me, a few years later, to redirect my goals toward something other than climbing. It took a while to sink in, but that was the epiphany.

Toward the end of the fourth day, we spied some rocks in the distance. We hadn't seen so much as a hill since leaving N'Djamena. Anticipation ran high. All of us were thinking, Will the rock be any good? When we got close enough, we piled out of the vehicles and literally ran over to the nearest formations.

We knew from Piero that the pinnacles and arches were made of sandstone. But would it be the sharp, clean sandstone of Nevada's Red Rocks, or chossy stuff like the Fisher Towers in Utah?

To our dismay, we discovered that the sandstone in the Ennedi ranged from terrible rock to truly atrocious, abominable rock. It was all bad. No matter what, however, the Ennedi was a photographer's and filmmaker's paradise, and the "media team" got images and footage like you see nowhere else in the world.

Our first major objective was a 200-foot-tall spire that we called the Citadel. As Mark described it, the tower was "shaped like a giant boxcar standing on end, featuring four distinct arêtes, one of which appeared to have decent holds. A rotten overhang guarded the bottom, but sported a crack that looked doable."

James Pearson was psyched to lead it. (I thought it looked like a death route.) He tied in and started up as Mark belayed, with the media team in rapt attention. I didn't want to just sit around and watch someone else climb—I hadn't come halfway around the world and four days across the desert just to spectate—so I wandered off and started soloing up a random nearby tower.

Before this trip, Tim, Jimmy, and Renan had seen me solo a little bit on solid rock, but Mark and James had never watched me solo at all. I think what I was doing now freaked them out a bit.

A CHARACTERISTIC HONNOLD understatement. In his essay about the Chad trip, Synnott wrote,

I heard a noise behind me and saw Honnold emerging, ropeless, from a bombay chimney 40 feet up a nearby tower. Above him rose an overhanging fist crack into which he set some jams, then swung his feet out of the chimney. Flowing like a snake up the rock, he was soon manteling over the lip. He built a small cairn and then down-soloed the tower via an overhanging face. On his way down, he broke off several hand and footholds, and I was barely able to watch. He later admitted that the downclimb had been a little more than he'd bargained for.

According to Synnott, Alex made some six solo first ascents of untouched routes during the time it took Pearson, climbing brilliantly, to get to the top of the Citadel.

Interviewed after the team's return from Chad, Jimmy Chin reported that when Alex was soloing, "It got so that we couldn't watch. And we also didn't want him to know we were watching, because we didn't want to give him any extra motivation to push it."

Several days after the Citadel climb, Alex started up—tied in, effectively toproping—on a beautiful sandstone arch. In his article, Synnott played this exploit up as zany hijinks:

We ended up one day sitting below a 100-foot-tall arch with a 180-degree rainbow offwidth crack splitting the underside of the formation. I had zero interest in climbing this heinous fissure, but Honnold was psyched. . . .

Ten feet off the ground, Honnold lunged for a basketball-sized hold that promptly exploded in his face, sending him winging across the arch. Once the route had spit him off, you could see in Honnold's face that it was "game on."

He jumped back on and for more than [an] hour, battled his way up, across, and then down the other side of the offwidth. He shuffled across the horizontal section by hanging upside down by foot cams. "That was the most disgusting route of my life," Honnold exclaimed, panting, his body covered in dust and bat piss, but with a huge grin on his face. He looked happier than I'd seen him all trip.

Yet four years later, Synnott looked back on Alex's free soloing in Chad with lingering misgivings, verging on disapproval. "In Chad," he says, "Alex was cavalier about risk. Over-confident. On that first tower, what he was doing was just plain mind-numbing. As he down-climbed, he broke loose three of his four holds, so he was dangling by one arm.

"'What was that all about?' I asked him when he got down. He didn't answer. He wouldn't cop to it.

"As far as I can tell, Alex came very close to falling off in the Ennedi."

Yeah, I've heard those guys' comments, but only second-hand. I think one thing that freaked them a little was the assumption that if you're going to free solo, you should do it on routes you've climbed before, even carefully rehearsed, so that there are no unwelcome surprises. As I had on Moonlight Buttress. To free solo rock that you've never touched before—a lot of it chossy and loose—might seem too out there.

But what I was soloing in Chad wasn't that hard—maybe 5.7. As for breaking off holds as I downclimbed that first tower, Mark's got it wrong. Yes, it was an overhanging wall, and I was hanging from two 5.5 mud jugs. Both my footholds broke off, but it wasn't hard to hang on, and I definitely wasn't dangling by one arm.

On a route called Royal Arches in Yosemite, I once pulled off a big hold on a 5.5 pitch I was soloing. My body swung backward, but I was able to grab the hold, shove it back in place, and recover. It was scary, but it was like magic. On 5.5, it's easy to have magic. On 5.11, it's not as magical.

We climbed for ten days in the Ennedi. The poor quality of the sandstone meant that bolts, and, for that matter, any of our gear, wouldn't really hold, which added a lot to the adventure of the climbing. Mark and James had real fears about ripping all the pro on a pitch, including the anchors. I found myself retreating off as many lines as I finished, though it didn't matter as much because it's easier to bail when soloing.

In the end, as I mentioned, it wasn't the climbing that made the trip so memorable. It was having an adventure in a completely alien landscape, and witnessing a way of life that would have been unimaginable to me beforehand. In Chad, I saw extreme poverty for the first time. It was hard for me to imagine living your whole life and never touching anything but sand. What we saw there were people surviving in a full-on Stone Age culture.

The trip coincided with a time when my own life was getting easier, thanks to sponsorship and recognition. Nowadays I can film a two-day commercial and make more money than those people in Chad make in their whole lives. That's fucked up. And that discrepancy ultimately forced me to examine how I ought to live my own life, and what I could do for others who were less fortunate.

B Y THE TIME ALEX WENT to Chad, in November 2010, he and Stacey were back together. But there would be subsequent breakups in their future. Looking back in 2014, Alex commented, "I find it really hard to see six months into the future, let alone a year or more. Stacey complains that that makes it hard for us to talk about our future together. She wants to know where we might live, or whether she should continue to work as a nurse, or just live with me on the road.

"We've talked about having children. I sort of joke that I'd like to have grandkids some day, but the thought of raising an infant seems heinous. Probably has something to do with my own childhood, but I don't really want to go there.

"It bugs Stacey when I joke about dying. I might say something like, 'You better appreciate me now, because I may not be around very long.' I'm just goofing around, but Stacey hates it. I know that she believes that I won't fall off soloing. She has faith in my ability and judgment.

"Some of our breakups got triggered by my feeling that I needed to be alone, that a relationship interfered with my climbing. When I told her that, she got really mad. She told me bluntly, 'Okay, it's over. Don't talk to me. Don't even try to contact me.'

"Then a few weeks or even months go by, and I realize I miss Stacey. I'll get all sheepish and call her up. 'I know you didn't want me to contact you,' I'll say, 'but couldn't we meet just to talk? Maybe have lunch?' She gives in, because I insist that I've learned more about myself and have realized that Stacey does have a positive impact on my life. And after all, we really do love each other."

In an unguarded moment, Alex admitted, "I think Stacey has had a lot to do with humanizing me." What spurred that insight was a playback in 2014 of some comments that Alex made to this writer [David Roberts] in 2010, when I interviewed him for a profile published in the May 2011 issue of *Outside* magazine.

An example. In 2010, Alex referred to having to go to North Carolina for a North Face appearance as "a gong show." He added, "I see all this stuff as media b.-s." An upcoming appearance as the featured speaker at the Banff Mountain Film and Book Festival was "full-on b.-s. I mean it's okay, but it's time I can't spend climbing."

"You want this on the record?" I asked.

"Why not?"

"How are your Banff hosts going to react if they read that comment?"

Alex shrugged. "I just say what I feel. Maybe it'll come back to bite me in the ass someday, and then I'll just stop talking to people."

Other comments in 2010 sounded like nonchalant bragging. "Yeah," said Alex, "I crushed high school. I took a test once, and they said I was a genius."

Yet others sounded like cruel putdowns, as when Alex dismissed one of America's leading female rock climbers as "a bit of a puss," because she'd had to ask her partner to overprotect a scary traverse she was seconding. About this high-profile climber, Alex added dismissively, "She hasn't done anything I couldn't do."

In 2010, Chris Weidner, one of Alex's best friends, complained, "When we started climbing together, he was very polite, very safety-conscious. Now, he's more likely to bad-mouth you. About a year ago, I was trying to lead this pitch, and I kept falling off. Alex said, 'Dude, what's your fucking problem? It's only five-thirteen.' He may have been joshing, but it hurt my feelings. He's got a certain attitude now, like, unless you're a world-class climber, you suck.

"I finally said, 'Hey, give me a break. I'm trying as hard as I can.' He may have realized he was hurting my feelings, but he just doesn't want to deal with it."

When I reminded Alex of these comments in 2014, he was abashed. "That's not me anymore," he insisted. "I think back then I was pretty aggro. I thought I had something to prove."

By 2015, Alex Honnold evidently has little still to prove. Yet his intensity shows no signs of ebbing. Something still drives him to a kind of perfection on rock—and recently, on snow and ice—that goes beyond the frontiers established by his boldest predecessors.

No matter what the difference in our styles and approaches—old-school versus new-school, mountaineer versus rock climber—Mark Synnott and I always got along well. Today I consider him one of my mentors, as well as one of the teammates I'm most indebted to. After Chad, I signed up for yet another Synnott trip sponsored by The North Face and Men's Journal. This time, in July 2011, we headed off for Devil's Bay on the south coast of Newfoundland, where big granite cliffs rise straight out of the ocean. We hoped to put up some good new routes there and document everything with camera and film.

Two others of our gang from the Chad expedition—James Pearson and Tim Kemple—were returning, and it was good to renew our friendship in Canada. The other three were Jim Surette, Matt Irving, and Hazel Findlay. I'd climbed a bit here and there with Hazel and Matt but had never met Jim, though Mark spoke highly of him. Hazel is a really strong British chick who evolved from gym climbing (six times British junior champion in indoor competitions) to become—a rare thing for women—a very strong trad leader on dangerous runout routes. Sender Films would make a beguiling film about her called Spice Girl, and I would later climb with Hazel in South Africa for another film, called Africa Fusion, released in 2015.

The only problem with the Newfoundland expedition was that the weather didn't cooperate. It turned out to be a miserable washout. To kill the downtime, I jotted down notes almost like I was writing a diary. Some entries:

It's been raining on and off for 10 days and everything in my small tent is getting a little damp. Though I'm the lucky one on the trip, everyone else on the team had their tents either destroyed or damaged in last night's freakishly strong wind storm. . . . So far we've *climbed one route and sat in the rain and brooded. Well, to be honest, I'm brooding and everyone else is drinking a lot and making the best of it.*

Before coming on this trip I felt like I was in great shape, climbing my first traditional 8b+ [5.14a] and a few other hard sport routes. I was fresh off a good season in Yosemite in which I'd soloed some things I was proud of. . . . Things should have been going great for me, and yet all I could think about while I festered in my damp tent was that my fitness was slipping away and that I was wasting my time. I could be anywhere else in the world, climbing every day. Instead, here I was in a tent, in the rain, depressed out of my mind.

I try to make the best of it and go for hikes despite the constant rain, just because the landscape is so beautiful. But then days of whiteout fog descend and it seems too dangerous to go wandering away from camp. I'm locked in my tent with nothing to do but read and do pushups.

We spend most of the time in the communal mess tent telling stories and bantering. Not that there's anything in particular to say after a week of rain, yet Mark has a distinctly entertaining way of telling sto- ries, even if I have heard them all at least twice before. In many ways our trip to Newfoundland is what people who work normal jobs do for vacation: go somewhere exotic with a group of friends and then hang out all day eating and drinking.

Several years later, looking back on our Newfoundland trip, Mark insisted that the expedition had been a success. He thought that we'd made a good short film by making "raininess" the central theme. It was titled Tent Bound in Devil's Bay.

Mark told other people that the rest of the guys had a running joke about me. That I would just sit in the group tent, muttering,

"This is the grimmest place on earth." Mark even called me a sort of Debbie Downer, almost a whiner. He thought I damaged the group's morale. He also thought that a route the team free climbed, called Leviathan, was "awesome."

Well, sorry, Mark, but that's not how I remember Devil's Bay. Tent Bound is a horrible little film, because the guys didn't have anything to work with. There was no story. James Pearson and I free climbed a route called Lucifer's Lighthouse, which was the hardest thing on the wall. But the whole trip was grim. Not just because of the rain. If you were in Patagonia, it'd be worth waiting out the weather, just to get a chance to climb on some of the most epic peaks on earth. But I'd just come from the Valley, and I was losing my fitness day after day. And this place sucked. Wet, slabby granite, not featured, not that tall . . . worse than the stuff in Tuolumne. I could have been doing this kind of climbing in Tuolumne and eating pizza every afternoon. Newfoundland just wasn't rad. It wasn't the future.

As for me being Debbie Downer, well, that's not entirely fair. Everybody was bummed and bored. I went on hikes, but then we'd get those impossible whiteouts. You could get lost in the fog. It was hard to find the latrine, a hundred feet from camp.

I was, I'll admit, the most vocal member of our crew, saying early on, "We should just leave."

But I don't hold any of this against Mark. Every trip I've gone on with him has been a life experience. I always learn something.

• • • •

Between my trips to Chad and Newfoundland, in the winter of 2010–11, I embarked on what I half-jokingly called my Sport Climbing Tour of the Antiquities. From Africa I went straight to Israel, then Jordan, then Turkey, then Greece. In Israel and Jordan, I stayed with a friend. Stacey joined me for Turkey and Greece.

It wasn't a true tourist vacation. I did all the hardest routes in Israel, and all the hardest routes at Geyikbayiri in Turkey. At Kalymnos in Greece, where the climbing is terrific, I got shut down somewhat because it had rained so much the limestone cliffs were seeping.

As for the antiquities, I actually read some books about the histories of the countries where I was climbing. I did all kinds of cultural stuff. Got a pretty legit taste of the past. Saw a lot of old things. Saw a lot of people in funny dress.

A trip like that serves as a kind of filler-in between real climbing adventures. I traveled, climbed, tried new things, learned new stuff, all while I was preparing for something big. Two thousand eleven, like 2009, was what I call a year of consolidation.

In Alex Lowther's profile of me for Alpinist (summer 2011), he writes about the pressure on me to keep upping the ante. He paraphrases the public's response to my big free solos: "What's next? Give us more!" And he adds,

> Expectations can be dangerous, and they only become more so when what you are famous for is risking your life.
>   If he's not careful, we could admire Alex Honnold to death.

That's a fair concern, but it's not like I haven't dealt with this pressure ever since folks started noticing what I was doing. The pressure only nudges me if it's about a project I want to do anyway. Actually, a bigger motivator than any media attention would be a hot chick at the base of a wall who I could impress. Though she probably couldn't tell the difference between 5.10 and 5.13. But no matter how hot the chick is, say if I was standing at the base of El Cap, and she urged me to free solo some route, my answer would be "No way."

For example, I can't tell you how many people over the years have pressured me to drink alcohol. We'll be at a party, and some-body will taunt me, "Alex, just try this beer, it's not gonna hurt you to take a sip." I've never given in. Booze doesn't interest me.

Most of the media attention that has come my way so far has been focused on my free solos. But that's not the only kind of climbing that compels me. Just as rad, in my book, are the big-wall linkups I've attempted, especially in Yosemite. And 2012 would be another watershed year for me, as I went after speed climbs on the big walls and linkups, both with partners and solo, of some of the most epic routes in North America.

CHAPTER **FIVE**
TRIPLE PLAY

Borneo, Chad, and even Newfoundland were novel experiences for me, but throughout my still relatively short climbing career, I keep coming back to the Valley when I want to push myself. Because of the sheer scale and difficulty of its soaring, clean granite walls, Yosemite offers almost limitless challenges to today's best climbers—as it will, I'm sure, to the stars of the next generation. No one, for example, has yet attempted a free solo of any of the routes on El Capitan.

One of the great landmarks in Valley history came in 1975, when three of the Stonemasters—Jim Bridwell, John Long, and Billy Westbay—pulled off the first one-day ascent of the Nose. The first route ever climbed on El Cap, the Nose was put up in 1958 in a monstrous siege effort stretching over forty-seven days by the legendary Warren Harding and a series of teammates. Bridwell, Long, and Westbay, climbing mostly free, surged up the route in about sixteen hours. There's a famous photo of the trio shot in the meadow below El Cap after the climb. To get the wall as well as the climbers in the frame, the photographer has hunkered down to the level of the guys' knees. Because of that angle, they seem to exude cockiness—gods sneering down on mere mortals. Cigarettes dangle from Bridwell's and Long's mouths. They're dressed like hippies, in loose-fitting vests and shirts, but they could just as well pass for Hell's Angels.

By the time I first hit the Valley, almost thirty years after that landmark ascent, climbing the Nose in a single day was still a pretty big deal. In 2010, I managed to do that three times, paired with Ueli Steck. We'd talked about trying to go for the speed record, which was then held by Hans Florine and Yuji Hirayama, at an amazing 2:37:05—yes, just a little over two and a half hours. But things didn't quite work out.

Instead, in early June 2010, I took a big step upward when I soloed the Nose, also in a single day.

As I mentioned above, no one has yet even attempted to free solo a route on El Cap. But there are other kinds of soloing that aren't quite so extreme. The distinctions may seem arcane to nonclimbers, but they're huge for those of us who go after big walls.

Rope soloing is a process in which you belay yourself, usually by tying one end of the rope to an anchor, the other end to your harness, then leading more or less conventionally, placing pro or clipping fixed gear as you go. Instead of a belayer to catch your fall, you minimize the potential plunge by using one of several different devices. I generally use a grigri, the same autolocking belay device that I use to catch a friend at the sport crag or gym, though in this case I'm using it to catch myself.

The trouble with rope soloing is that it's extremely tedious. You have to negotiate each pitch three times to make progress—leading it with pro, rappelling to "clean" (retrieve) the pro, then "jugging" back up the rope (climbing the line itself with ascenders, metal devices that grip the rope under a downward pull but slide easily upward). Way back in 1971, Peter Haan climbed the Salathé route on El Cap—along with the Nose, one of its two most storied lines—in a monumental rope-soloing effort spread across six days. Haan used some kind of combination of prusik knot and Jumar (then the most popular ascender) to belay himself. What's pretty amazing is that he had never done a big wall before. I don't know Haan, but I can appreciate how rad his exploit seemed in its day.

In 2010, when I soloed the Nose, I carried a thin sixty-meter rope in my pack only because I knew there were a few pitches that I'd have to rope solo. They included the King Swing, a massive pendulum that allows you to escape from the apparent dead end of the Boot Flake. I lowered myself from my anchor a hundred feet, then started running and scrabbling sideways across blank granite, so that I could build up longer and longer swings. Finally I was able to grab the edge of a crack far to the left that leads to the crack system that continues the route. It's quite a daunting maneuver to pull off solo. The King Swing is like the biggest pendulum in climbing. At least it's the biggest one I've ever done.

It was a tough trade-off to burden myself with the weight of a sixty-meter rope that I'd use only a few times on the Nose, but I doubt that I could have gotten up the route without it. Most of the time, what I was doing was daisy soloing.

A daisy chain is a loop of nylon webbing, a little longer than an arm's reach, that's sewn into as many as a dozen regularly spaced miniloops. You keep one end firmly attached to your harness, then you clip whichever miniloop is at the right length to a cam or nut you've placed or a piton or bolt that's already in place. Then you can hang safely on aid from the gear, or just use it as a handhold to get past a tricky move. I carried two daisies, so that I could alternate clips without ever interrupting the security of my static connection to good pro. On the very hardest aid pitches on the Nose, like the crux of a big overhang called the Great Roof (rated

5.13d), I used the daisies to hang from either cams I placed or fixed gear—some of it pretty old and nearly worthless.

During most of the climb on the Nose, however—all but the very hardest passages—I was truly free soloing. The transition from daisy soloing to free is scary. I have to constantly remind myself, Now I'm safe. Now I'm not. It's tough mentally. But you never forget, never think you're clipped to pro when you're actually attached to nothing. You're fully aware during those long stretches when only your hands and feet finding the right holds keep you from taking the big plunge.

Even though by 2010 I'd already free soloed Half Dome and Moonlight Buttress, the feats that seemed to put me on the climbing map, this daisy solo of the Nose felt like a big deal for me. I was proud of how efficiently I climbed, too, since the whole ascent took me only five hours and fifty minutes.

Still, I had even grander ambitions for Yosemite that season.

• • • •

When I was still a young gym rat in Sacramento, I saw a film called Masters of Stone 5. One episode covered the daisy-solo linkup by Dean Potter of the Nose on El Cap and the Regular Northwest Face on Half Dome in a single day—Potter's elapsed time was twenty-three hours and twenty-three minutes. I thought, That is fucking cool. Just the idea of climbing two big walls in a single day filled me with awe.

Dean has since become a friend of mine, but back then he was a role model and an idol, both for his speed climbs and his audacious free solos. He's thirteen years older than me. We've bouldered together a few times but never gotten to climb anything big. Unfortunately, the media have tried to paint us as rivals, with him as the aging guru being challenged by me, the young upstart.

Anyway, after climbing the Nose with Ueli Steck in May and June 2010, I had the moves pretty well dialed. And I thought the Regular Northwest Face on Half Dome should be pretty mellow if I used daisies to protect myself at the hard parts—the sequences that had scared me two years earlier, when I'd free soloed the route.

Late on June 21, I headed up the long approach to the base of Half Dome, planning to bivouac there and get started at first light. Somehow, though, I mistimed the sunrise, waking up at 4:45 a.m. and having to sit around waiting for the lights to come on. I had a minimal rack and a thirty-foot line that I use to tow my van, which I figured could work for the Robbins Traverse—the only time I expected to use a rope.

Once it got light, I scrambled up the huge snow cone at the base of the wall—still there in June, courtesy of an unusually heavy winter. Halfway up the first pitch, I changed into climbing shoes and switched to rock-climbing mode, after tossing down my jacket and headlamp. I had a small pack with my shoes, food, and water, figuring it was important for me to stay well fed and hydrated since I was going to have a long day.

The climbing itself was pretty uneventful. It felt mostly moderate, compared to my free solo two years before—especially since I used the bolt ladders to avoid the hard free climbing, the same bolt ladders I'd had to detour around in 2008 to keep my free solo pure. Farther up, I climbed the chimneys with my pack hanging down below me on a daisy. The only time I really had to pay attention was on the Zig-Zags, where I climbed with two pieces clipped to my daisies on all the hard parts. As it turned out, I never used my thirty-foot towline.

The final slab, which had been quite stressful for me free soloing two years before, felt totally casual. Instead of insecure friction moves on almost invisible footholds, I could just pull on the bolts and swing between them on my daisies when need be. It was an entirely different experience.

I topped out among a handful of hikers. It was about 7:00 a.m. and the summit was still quite peaceful, a pleasant change from the usual gong show. I savored my climb for a few minutes while eating some food, then started my descent.

I'd timed the climb at two hours and nine minutes, which made it a new solo speed record for the route. It's sort of funny, but I can convince myself that speed for its own sake isn't a high priority for me. On Thank God Ledge, for instance, I wasted ten minutes trying to "booty" a brand-new #4 Camalot that somebody had recently gotten stuck in a crack. Just the day before, I'd learned a trick about hitting the individual lobes a certain way and walking cams around. I wanted to make it work. But after a while I gave up. For all I know, the Camalot is still there.

On the way down from Half Dome, I stopped to look at two amazing birds. I hate to have to hurry. The whole timing thing, I've claimed in print, is not a strong point for me.

Yet if that were really true, why did I time my ascent? Why was it important for me—not only on that day, but on many climbs thereafter—to go after speed records? I suppose it all comes back to purism. A speed record on a big wall is the ultimate validation that I've climbed as efficiently as I know how. It's consistent with my philosophy of life, my emphasis on simplicity, on paring away extraneous stuff. I also like speed records because they give a baseline for improvement. It's nice to know that I can improve on a route. It's gratifying to find that I can go faster.

From the summit of Half Dome, I hustled down to Mirror Lake, where I'd stashed a bike, then rode it back to my van. I reached El Cap Meadow around 10:00 a.m. There I spent some time reracking and trying to eat and drink. I didn't really know what I would need on the Nose, so I went a little heavy on gear: pretty much a double rack of cams. I had a skinny rope that I'd borrowed from a friend, something like an 8.5 millimeter. I figured it would be enough for my purposes. I wasn't planning on whipping huge on it.

All told, my gear weighed more than I would have liked. I hadn't really thought about it beforehand, but the problem with soloing is that you carry everything, all the time. Climbing with a partner, normally you burn off the rack as you go, so by the end of the pitch you only have a little left. And conversely, the rope weighs nothing at the beginning of a pitch. But when you're daisy soloing, you have the whole weight of everything on you all the time.

At the foot of the Nose, there were a bunch of parties converging from different directions. Some Frenchmen who were hauling bags, some Russians who were only hoping to climb to Sickle Ledge (a mere four pitches up) to check it out, some Americans who were at the very bottom and said they were taking up a lot of beer. I was a little weirded out by the whole show and took off climbing as soon as I could. I felt super self-conscious to start free soloing up a crack that people were lined up to aid climb.

It was surreal to look up the Nose and think that I would be scrambling the whole thing by myself. I had a good supply of food and water as well as a headlamp. I was prepared for anything, though I was planning on climbing in the same style as I had on Half Dome. Free soloing everything I could and daisy soloing anything hard. I had the rope for a few pendulums, the King Swing, and the Great Roof.

Everything went smoothly on the first three pitches, which seemed easier than I expected. On the fourth pitch, I got a pleasant surprise. Someone had fixed an extremely bomber line up across the two tricky pendulums to Sickle Ledge. I could see that the rope was fixed to the bolt on Sickle and refixed to a half-dozen pieces along its way down, so I happily hand-over-handed up and saved myself a lot of ropework. I figured that something useful like that makes up for all the times that you go up on a pitch and discover that someone has cleaned all the fixed gear or ripped a crucial piece that's supposed to be left in place, either by falling and pulling it out or by deliberately scavenging it. And then sometimes you get lucky and find a rope left in place!

Dolt Tower, ten pitches up, was my first real stop. It was time to eat and drink again, and I checked my timer. It read something like 1:15, which was a pretty damn good pace. I realized that I wouldn't be needing a headlamp after all. I waved down to the meadow, knowing that my friend Tom Evans was probably watching on his telescope, and I wondered if any of my other friends were around. Then I took a leak and wondered if they watched that, too. I figured if they could see everything from down in the meadow, then I had nothing to be ashamed of. . . .

I rope soloed the short aid section up to the Boot Flake, but then I took myself off belay before I free soloed the actual Boot itself. It's simpler for me not to deal with a rope, especially on something secure like a hand crack. Still, it's exciting to take yourself off belay on El Cap.

Everything went uneventfully up to the Great Roof, which is where I planned to do my only full pitch of traditional rope soloing. I'd even brought a single Jumar for the occasion. This was one of my first real pitches of rope soloing ever, but it went smoothly. I started to notice how tired I felt as I jugged, so I told myself I wouldn't do any more rope soloing. From here to the top, I was going to daisy solo, even if it took longer. I couldn't bear to go up and down to clean pitches.

At the base of the Pancake Flake, I put my rope in my pack. That was one of the more memorable moments of the day. As I unclipped my daisies from the anchor and started free soloing the easy lieback above me, I felt absolutely heroic. The sheer exposure of twenty-three pitches dropping off beneath me filled me with glee. I'd spent a lot of the season posing for photos on various routes for a couple of different projects. Now I found myself doing the most exposed climbing of my life all alone. It was invigorating.

The last six pitches are mostly hand cracks, so I largely free soloed them, but I was getting more and more tired. I started grabbing fixed gear a little more—"French freeing," we sardonically call it, after the traditional style in the Alps. As I climbed into the Changing Corners, I passed into the shade, which brought me new life. Climbing in the full sun all afternoon had left me a little wilted, and my feet hurt from hot, tight climbing shoes. And then, on the last two pitches, I finally caught up to the parties I'd seen from the base. I stopped at an anchor to eat some food and chitchat with a cute belayer. But as much as I felt like hanging out and chilling in the shade, I still had to get to the top. So I climbed through the leader, with permission of course, and didn't stop again until the summit.

I was massively psyched to reach the top. My timer said 5:50, but I rounded up to six hours, since I hadn't started it until the top of the first pitch. I'd been distracted by the mob at the base and hadn't remembered to start the timer.

Now I couldn't quite believe that I'd actually done the linkup, and in roughly half a day. Having thought about it with awe for so long, I found it a little surreal to actually do it.

Honestly, I don't remember anything about the hike down or what I did on the ground. I guess none of that stuff was as important to me as the actual climbing. Weird that I can remember individual placements I used on the Glowering Spot, but I can't remember where I went for dinner, or with who.

A LEX'S LINKUP OF Half Dome and the Nose had taken him only a little over eleven hours, including hiking down from Half Dome and biking, driving, and hiking to the foot of El Cap. That was less than half the time of Dean Potter's daisy-solo linkup in 2002, the feat that had first inspired Alex to "go big" (one of his favorite mottoes). Of course a decade in Yosemite is an eternity in terms of speed climbing on the classic routes. Between 1991 and 2002, for instance, the speed record on the Nose—achieved by roped pairs simul-climbing, or moving at the same time without belays—dropped from six hours and one minute to two hours and forty-nine minutes.

Still, Alex was justly proud that on his June 2010 marathon day he'd set not only the solo speed record for both routes but also the speed record for the linkup, with or without a partner. Yet this formidable accomplishment didn't generate the kind of buzz that had greeted Alex's free solos of Moonlight Buttress and Half Dome. The climbing magazines paid him dutiful homage: *Alpinist* cadged what its editor called "a characteristically nonchalant e-mail" out of Alex, summarizing his big day in the Valley. Stewart Green, a prolific commentator on the climbing scene, tipped his cap: "It's hard to know what to make of Alex's astounding ascents. No words can describe the difficulty and dangerousness of these ascents. It's simply pure brashness. Let's face it—the kid has a lot of chutzpah. Climb high, Alex, and be safe."

Alex's Valley nickname—Alex "No Big Deal" Honnold—helps explain the muted response to his pathbreaking linkup. The narrative he wrote a few weeks after the climb for Black Diamond, one of his sponsors, is short on gee-whiz superlatives and long on phrases such as "pretty uneventful," "easier than expected," and "totally casual."

Throughout his career, it's been a source of mild amusement

to Alex that the public goes gaga over his free soloing but seems to undervalue his massive linkups on big walls at record paces. Of course, for a nonclimbing audience, the stark simplicity of free soloing—if you fall, you die—comes across instantly in a few seconds of video footage. It's a lot harder for that audience to grasp the rigors of daisy soloing, especially the way Alex performs it, with the grueling mental ballet of switching constantly, as he puts it, from *Now I'm safe* to *Now I'm not*. The unspoken fallacy beneath a casual observer's take on one of Alex's bold daisy solos is that because he clips in to fixed gear or to cams he places on all the hardest parts, he's taken the extreme challenge out of the game. Nothing could be further from the truth. And though he can say, "I hate to have to hurry," Alex strives for speed on the big walls, even as he has to make shrewd calculations as to which pitches he will free solo and which he will cruise with his daisy chains. For that matter, even trusting your life to a fixed piton can be a gamble, as some of the pro placed years ago has weathered out and can no longer safely support a climber's weight, let alone a leader fall.

After his record-setting double, Alex still wasn't through with Yosemite linkups. The ultimate prize, he knew, was the Yosemite Triple—back-to-back climbs not only of El Cap and Half Dome but also of the south face of Mount Watkins. Those three walls stand as the biggest trio in the Valley. To enchain them would require not only technical perfection but the stamina of a world-class distance runner.

Once again, the role model showing Alex the way was Dean Potter, who in 2001, climbing with Timmy O'Neill, scaled all three walls in a single day. On their linkup, Potter and O'Neill mixed free climbing with "French free," aiding on pro to surmount the hardest stretches. It was a landmark achievement, pushing the boundaries of what in 2001 was considered possible. (Even today, the authoritative site Supertopo.com lists "normal" times on the south face of Mount

Watkins as two to three days, three days for the Regular Northwest
Face on Half Dome, and five days for the Nose on El Cap.)

By the spring of 2012, Alex was back in Yosemite. This time he
would pair up with another of his role models, Tommy Caldwell.
Despite Caldwell's being seven years older than Alex, the two would
soon form one of those rare partnerships destined to make climbing
history, like the French duo of Lionel Terray and Louis Lachenal in
the 1940s and '50s or the German brothers Alex and Thomas Huber
in the 1990s and 2000s. Each would bring out the best in the other,
complementing one another's particular strengths as climbers. And
they got along like great friends just hanging out and having a good
time, even when they were in the midst of a serious battle.

Even as a teenager *in Sacramento, I was aware of Tommy
Caldwell's stellar record in big-wall climbing. He seemed to spe-
cialize in first free ascents of routes on El Cap, including the Dihedral Wall and Magic Mushroom, both rated 5.14a. Yet he'd also
excelled as a sport climber, solving a short route called Flex Luthor
at the Fortress of Solitude in Colorado—rated a possible 5.15a,
which remained throughout my childhood the hardest single route
climbed in the United States. And in 2006, on his first trip to Patagonia, Tommy and two partners made the first free ascent of a
beautiful route on Fitz Roy called Línea de Eleganza. (The first
ascent, with heavy reliance on aid and fixed ropes, took an Italian
party nine days. Tommy's team onsighted every pitch and got up
the wall in only two days.)*

*I think a big key to Tommy's success is his incredible work ethic.
He'll hike four hours to a route, then spend eight hours working
it in the rain. Or he'll haul huge loads to the top of El Cap, then
rap down just to check out a potential project. By the fall of 2014,*

Tommy had been trying for seven straight years to complete the first free ascent of the Dawn Wall on El Cap, which he knew would be the hardest big wall free climb in the world. I could only imagine the tenacity and drive it would take to work on a single route nearly every season for most of a decade. I don't think I'd have the patience for such a long-term challenge.

Tommy's also had some experiences you wouldn't wish on anybody. In 2000, at the age of twenty-three, with his girlfriend (and later wife), Beth Rodden, as well as two other climbing buddies, Tommy was forced off a big wall in Kyrgyzstan when terrorists shot bullets at the climbers' portaledge a thousand feet off the deck. Once on the ground, the four were taken prisoner and then forced for days to march and hide as their captors evaded army soldiers hunting them. An unfortunate soldier whom the terrorists had also captured was executed just out of sight of their bivouac. Tommy, Beth, and their two teammates believed they would be executed themselves. They succeeded in escaping one night when Tommy pushed off a cliff the sole terrorist charged with guarding them. (Amazingly, the guy survived, only to be captured by the army and imprisoned under a death sentence.) The four young climbers then ran for the government front line, coming close to getting shot at by mistake. The whole wild adventure is chronicled in Greg Child's dramatic book Over the Edge.

The very next year, 2001, Tommy accidentally cut off his left index finger with a table saw. That kind of mishap can end a climbing career. Tommy had the finger sewed back on, but when it simply got in the way of his climbing, he had it removed. Today, at age thirty-seven, he's climbing as well as he ever has, despite the missing digit.

So I had always admired Tommy from a distance, but when we started climbing together, it was a joy to discover what a kind, generous, unegotistical guy he is. Unlike some professional athletes,

Tommy never toots his own horn, and, as a result, I think he's gotten less credit for what he's done than he deserves.

In May 2012, Tommy's idea for the Yosemite Triple—the south face of Mount Watkins, a route called Freerider on El Cap that weaves in and out of the standard Salathé line, and the Regular Northwest Face on Half Dome—was not simply to pull off the linkup in a single day but to free climb every single foot of all three routes. I knew that would be a tall order, but I was psyched to give it a shot with such a strong and motivated partner.

We started up Watkins at 4:45 p.m. on May 18. It was already hot in the Valley, so we arranged our schedule to maximize time in the shade. The technique we all use nowadays for speed climbing big walls is called simul-climbing. It works like this. One guy takes the rack and leads continuously, not for a single pitch but for as much as 800 or even a thousand feet. He doesn't stop to belay. Once the rope comes tight to the second, he starts up, too. Both guys climb simultaneously—hence "simul-climbing." The leader places cams or nuts every so often, or clips fixed gear, so that if either guy falls, the gear catches them in a kind of yo-yo effect, when the rope comes tight between them. You can take some pretty horrendous whippers simul-climbing and still not get hurt, as long as the pro is good.

Ironically, the most dangerous situation in simul-climbing arises when the second falls. If the leader falls, the rope coming tight to the second arrests the plunge, the second acting as a kind of unwitting anchor. But if the second falls, he can pull off the leader. Not good if both guys are falling at once, no matter how good your pro!

But part of what allowed Tommy and me to climb the Triple was using devices like the Kong Duck or the Petzl Micro Traxion, single-directional pulleys that allow the rope to go one way but not the other. When placed strategically, they allow the second to climb through terrain that would otherwise be considered much too hard—too close to the edge of falling off. Tommy and I could climb such big blocks—sometimes over a thousand feet at a time—because the devices made it safe for the second to climb as hard as 5.12.

Tommy and I led in what we call blocks—big stretches covering as many as twelve or thirteen conventional pitches of, say, eighty to 150 feet each. It's inevitable that as the leader places pro, he's going to run through his rack at some point. That's when you change over and give the rack and the lead to the other guy. We planned beforehand the places where our blocks would end, on ledges where a pendulum or a downclimb or some other unusual maneuver meant you had to manage the rope more carefully than in normal simul-climbing.

We got up Watkins in the excellent time of two hours and forty minutes. Neither of us took a single fall, despite pitches as hard as 5.13a. From there, a combination of hiking, driving, eating, and rehydrating got us to the foot of Freerider at 10:45 p.m. As we'd planned, we hoped to cruise all of El Cap in the dark. That's not quite as hard as it might seem, as long as you have the route sufficiently dialed so that your headlamp illuminates all the sequences and you don't get off-route.

In some ways, Freerider on El Cap was the climax of our adventure. One of the most memorable moments came in the wee hours. Tommy was leading up one of the harder corners. As he left his anchor, he said, "I'm too tired to lieback it, I'm just going to stem it," and then he proceeded to just totally bust out the entire pitch. I didn't even think you could do that! It's the middle of the night and it's really hard to see your feet because it's dark, he has a headlamp, he's standing on tiny little footholds that you wouldn't even be able to see in the light, and he just stemmed it, one foot on each slab, trusting those minuscule holds.

Tommy's a technical wizard on that stuff. He's really, really good on granite, so it was cool seeing how he could improvise like that and get away with it.

We got to the top of El Cap just after 5:00 a.m., with the first light of dawn. We'd finished Freerider in 6:15, also a damn good time. Tommy fell twice on the crux face climbing section, but no harm done, since I was belaying him, not simul-climbing. I managed not to come off anywhere.

Our big enemy was fatigue, and it really hit us on Half Dome. Having to free climb 5.12+ after twenty-one straight hours on the walls takes it out of you. It's really hard, and the prospect of failure—even if it meant "cheating" and using aid or grabbing fixed gear—is always there. The 5.12c variations on the Regular Northwest Face gave us all we could handle.

Each of the three routes has a specific crux. When we got to them we would get all psyched up, but they were all reasonable. The real trial is an overall, cumulative ordeal. Your feet hurt more and more and you get more and more tired. Linkups aren't super fun. Once you hit hour twelve or fourteen, you aren't really thinking, "Oh! What a great time we're having!" You think it will be cool until it isn't fun anymore.

It was 2:00 p.m. on May 19 when we topped out on Half Dome. Our elapsed time was twenty-one hours and fifteen minutes. Not only a new speed record but also the first free linkup of the three great Yosemite faces.

I was pretty pleased that I had managed to climb 7,000 feet of steep granite—seventy guidebook pitches—without falling once. And I'm equally gratified that, as of 2015, nobody else had duplicated our free linkup, no matter how long they took to do it.

As MONUMENTAL AN ACHIEVEMENT as Yosemite's Triple Crown with Caldwell was, Alex regarded it in some sense as a warm-up. His goal for months had been to try the Triple solo—not free climbing every pitch, but rope soloing and daisy soloing. As he would later claim, "Doing the Triple with Tommy, I knew, would actually be physically harder than daisy soloing it. After all, climbing 5.12+ when you're tired is way harder than French freeing the same pitch. By doing it free with Tommy, I learned just how tired I'd be when I got to Half Dome on a solo linkup."

After the success of *Alone on the Wall*, Peter Mortimer and Sender Films had stayed in close touch with Alex. Now, for a new film, to be titled *Honnold 3.0*, the filmmakers offered to shoot Alex's attempt on the solo Triple. For Mortimer and company, it would present a new kind of challenge. They would capture Alex's climb not in staged reenactments, as they had his free solos of Moonlight Buttress and Half Dome, but "in real time," as he attempted the linkup through a very long day and night. There would be no second takes, no rehearsals. If the camera missed a crucial bit of action, that would be too bad.

Logistically, such a shoot posed a fiendish challenge. The cameramen would have to rappel into positions on the three walls well before Alex got there, then simply hang out and wait for his arrival. To ensure Alex's comfort level, Mortimer chose shooters who not only were top-notch climbers but also were good friends with Alex. They included Ben Ditto, Cheyne Lempe, Mikey Schaefer, Sean Leary, and Mortimer himself.

Yet in Mortimer's view, such a project was actually less stressful than the shooting of *Alone on the Wall* had been. As he reflects today, "There was a cleaner ethical boundary for me. Worst-case scenario: If Alex wants to climb something and he falls off and dies, that's still his choice. But if he dies during a reenactment, then in some way I'd feel that I killed Alex. I'd have to live with that."

Even so, every shoot with Alex took its toll on the filmmakers. In June 2011, to provide footage for the *60 Minutes* interview with Alex, Mortimer had agreed to film another free solo in Yosemite. As a side project, the day before the big show, Alex chose to go after the Phoenix, a single 130-foot pitch, but one rated a solid 5.13a. It's a climb you have to rappel to reach the start, since it hangs over a sheer precipice looming more than 500 feet above the valley floor.

Mortimer had misgivings. As he recalls, "I was almost at the point of telling Alex, 'No more reenactments.' But he said, 'I'm gonna fucking do the Phoenix tomorrow morning. You wanna come?'

"'Do you want me there?'

"'Sure.'"

The next day, Mortimer got in position. "I zoomed in on him with my camera," he remembers. "What I saw brought home the reality of what he was holding onto. It was incredibly stark. The rock was overhanging, his feet were on nothing. The granite looked slippery from spray from a nearby waterfall. He had only three fingertips in shallow cracks.

"I was terrified. It was the scariest thing in my life. I couldn't handle watching up close, so I had to zoom out."

Alex cruised up the Phoenix in eight minutes flat. It was the first 5.13 route ever free soloed in Yosemite.

Mortimer tells another story, this time about cameraman Brett Lowell shooting Alex on a free solo on a route on Liberty Cap, a dome also in the Valley, for Sender's film *Valley Uprising*. "Brett had a fancy new camera. He was all set in position. Alex climbed up to him, then, only a few feet away from the camera, he set out from a locker crack onto a steep slab. Normally child's play for Alex. But he botched the sequence. Went up, downclimbed, went back up.

"Brett came close to losing it. He thought, *I'm going to film this guy falling to his death.* He turned white as a ghost. Alex noticed Brett's distress, and, in the middle of sorting out the moves, said, 'Hey, no big deal. This is what you do when you're climbing.'"

Yes, the logistics of filming *my Triple solo for the Sender guys were supercomplicated. But their presence actually made it easier and more pleasant for me. Daisy soloing requires a way lower commitment than free soloing, so it didn't really matter to me if other people were around, because I have a harness and a rope and I can just hang out. If I was free soloing and there was a cameraman next to me, it would be harder to focus. But it's nice to have friends around when you're climbing through the night.*

Also, the crew made my own logistics a lot easier. If I was alone, I'd have to figure out car shuttles between the climbs—a big hassle. But with the filmmakers, I had rides already set up. And they could give me food and water on the summits. If I was doing it alone, I would have pre-stashed food and water at various places along the route.

I started up the south face of Mount Watkins at 4:00 p.m. on June 5, 2012. The first pitches were a little wet and buggy, because it had rained the day before, but I felt pretty smooth. Finished the wall in 2:20, twenty minutes faster than Tommy and I had done it two weeks earlier.

It was kind of chaotic driving down to the start of El Cap. There was all this shit on the floor of the van—the filmmakers' Pelican cases, assorted gear of my own, since I'd use a different rack for El Cap, and I'm trying to eat and hydrate. And it was dark by now. I started up the Nose at 9:30 p.m. I got 150 feet up and realized I'd forgotten my chalk bag. Must have left it among the debris on the floor of the van. Oh, shit, I said to myself. I considered scrambling back down to get the bag, but by then the van had left. So I just climbed on without chalk. The lower pitches were wet, so I found it a little bit hard and weird.

Climbing in the dark is quieter and lonelier than in the day-light. In some ways, there's no exposure. You're inside this little bubble with your headlamp. A fifteen-foot beam of light is the whole universe. There was no danger I'd get off-route, since I knew the sequences so well by now. And yet, you still sense that there's this void below you, somewhere in the darkness. It's like swimming in the ocean and realizing there's a bottomless abyss below you.

When I got to the Dolt Tower, about a thousand feet up, I met two parties: one was a pair of guys bivouacking, the other two were cooking a meal. We exchanged pleasantries, then I asked, a bit sheepishly, "Do you guys have a chalk bag I could borrow?" This guy named Steve Denny unhesitatingly handed over his. It was a new felt bag, and it was full of chalk. Putting my hand into it felt orgasmic. I thanked Steve and told him I'd tie the bag to a tree on the summit, so he could retrieve it later. Then I headed on.

A strange thing about climbing in the dark is that all these crea-tures come out. Bugs, mice, bats, even frogs that live in the cracks. And these giant centipedelike insects. I've always worried that I'd step on one and splooge off. Then, all of a sudden, I heard this loud "whoosh!" and a scream. I nearly peed my pants. It took a moment to realize it had to be a BASE jumper. In fact, it was a friend of mine—I won't name him here, since BASE jumping is illegal in the park, which was why he flew at night.

At the Great Roof, I met up with Stanley—Sean Leary is his real name, but everybody calls him Stanley. After filming me on the roof, he climbed with me the rest of the way up the Nose, Jumar-ing next to me as I daisy soloed. We actually chatted about other things, such as the speed record on the Nose, which he was keen to go after. I didn't have to concentrate too hard, except for spots here and there where I'd say, "Hold on a moment. I need to focus."

Finished the Nose at 3:30 a.m., still in pitch dark. Six hours for the climb, fifteen minutes faster than Tommy and I had climbed Freerider.

The psychological crux of the whole linkup was actually on the grueling hike up to Half Dome, where I started to bonk. I felt agonizingly slow on the route, but I knew I was in the home stretch. Near the top, I ran into Mike Gauthier, who was chief of staff in the park and, unlike most of the rangers, a good climber. (Traditionally, in Yosemite there's been a constant antagonism between rangers and climbers.) He was roped up with a guy from the Access Fund—a nonprofit devoted to preserving access to climbing areas across America. We sort of climbed side by side a couple of pitches together. I hadn't met Mike before, but he seemed like a really nice dude. I thought it was cool—an NPS bigshot who was a serious climber, an Access Fund partner, and all that. Then I pushed on.

I topped out at 10:55 a.m. to a whole gong show of hikers on the summit. I was really tired, and the scene felt weird, out of control. My total time was 18:55. It was another speed record, but mainly I just felt psyched to have done it.

Four days later, when he topped out, Steve Denny recovered his chalk bag, which I'd tied to a tree.

*H*ONNOLD 3.0, WHICH SENDER packaged with four other films for its Reel Rock 7 anthology, released in 2012, is every bit as skillful and impressive as *Alone on the Wall*. The Yosemite Triple solo takes up only a little more than half the film, but it forms its inevitable climax. Picking up where the earlier feature ended, and segueing through Alex's appearance on *60 Minutes* and his role in a clever Citibank commercial, in which he belays Katie Brown (a former infatuation of Alex's) on a sandstone tower in Utah, the film poses the question of whether fame might corrupt or endanger Alex. As his good friend Cedar Wright puts it, "How do you do this when it becomes a public spectacle?"

The footage covering the Triple solo smoothly intercuts action sequences with friends as talking heads and Alex's own voice-overs. Anticipating the linkup, Wright pronounces, "If he pulls it off, it's the most monumental feat of soloing in Yosemite history."

On Watkins, the camera powerfully captures the scary dance of switching from daisy solo to free solo, especially where the bolts are far enough apart that Alex must unclip and climb a stretch without a safety net before he can clip in again. The alternation of "Now I'm safe. Now I'm not" comes across vividly. In voice-over, Alex says, "I guess I should have a disclaimer on this, because basically you should not do this, even though I love it and I think it's so fun." He grins at the paradox.

A thousand feet up the south face, there's a film moment that's already become as famous as the freakout on Thank God Ledge in *Alone on the Wall*. Free soloing, Alex traverses toward the camera, which is less than a dozen feet away. There's a bolt he hopes to clip. In the frame, you can't see either Alex's feet or the fingers that clasp a sloping ledge high above his head. He lets go with his left hand and reaches toward the bolt to measure how far away it is. His fingers stop an inch or two short of the bolt, but he knows he can clip it with a daisy. Carefully he reaches back to his harness, seizes the daisy, and puts the middle loops of it between his teeth as he reaches down for the biner.

All at once Alex's whole body jerks downward several inches. It's obvious that his foot has slipped off its hold. How had he kept his purchase on the wall, with only the fingers of his right hand gripping the out-of-sight sloping ledge? How close had he come to the fatal fall everyone worries he'll someday take?

Audiences invariably gasp, or even shriek out loud, at this moment. But on film, Alex's face registers nothing. He reaches down again, clasps the biner, clips it to the bolt, then swings across with his weight on the daisy. *Now I'm safe.*

When asked how Alex had felt about that terrifying close call, Mortimer later reported, "He didn't even remember it. But later, he gave me grief about it. He said, 'How come with all the great footage you got on the Triple, you put that single clip up on YouTube?'"

According to Alex, "In that moment, I wasn't even close to falling off. I had a really good handhold. The foot that slipped was not on a weight-bearing hold. I didn't want to lurch for the bolt. That wouldn't look good on camera."

Yet in the film, Alex's voice-over immediately after the slip on Watkins seems to acknowledge a close call. "Having little things go wrong," he says. "That's just part of the game. Those kinds of things shake you for a second, but then you just keep climbing."

Of necessity, because of the widely scattered positions where the cameramen had stationed themselves on the three walls, the film could not cover all the highlights of the linkup. Because there was no way cinematically to recount the drama of the forgotten chalk bag, Sender simply ignored it—even though there's footage of Alex gearing up with rack and rope in the dark as he heads toward El Cap.

Some of the best footage documents Alex climbing up the Nose in the dark, with the cone of his headlamp bathing the microworld of hand- and footholds, the void an inky blackness all around him. And fortuitously, at the Great Roof, the audio captures the "whoosh!" and joyous shout of the BASE jumper. A voice-over about the crux moves on the Great Roof perfectly complements the visuals. "The fixed nuts are hanging half out," Alex comments, "and they pull straight down, so it looks like it's all going to fall out. There's always running water, and slime coming out of [the crack]. It's a pretty intimidating position."

By accompanying Alex not only to the top of El Cap but also on the arduous approach up the "Death Slabs" to the foot of Half Dome, Sean Leary captures the extreme fatigue and dispirited mood of Alex as he gets ready for the last wall. He complains about the cold and looks as though all he wants to do is go to sleep. In voice-over, Alex admits feeling out of it on the "trudge" up the first half of the route. Then, miraculously, he finds his groove again. The last few hundred feet of climbing look effortless and triumphant.

The film ends with the "gong show" on top. Dozens of hikers, knowing he's near the top, lean over the edge of the precipice. "He's coming," one voice intones, and another, "That's so sick."

As Alex sits exhausted on the flat bedrock summit, hikers ask to take his picture and shake his hand. If he thinks the scene is weird, it doesn't show. Gracefully, he assents to their requests, shakes their hands, poses for a group photo with four awestruck teenage girls.

The final voice-over is a winning one. "I think of all the people who inspired me as a kid," Alex reflects, "and I sort of realize they were all normal people, too. I just do my normal life, and if people choose to be inspired by the things I'm doing, then I'm glad they're getting something out of it."

· · · ·

In the short span of two months, 2012 had already become a breakthrough year for Alex. But even after the Triple Crown solo, he still had one more project in his sights for Yosemite that season. Less than two weeks after topping out on Half Dome, Alex would enter the fiercest Valley competition of all—the race to set a new speed record on the Nose.

I can only guess what's going on here, but I look like I'm having a good time.
(Credit: Dierdre Wolownick)

Just playing around at the Gunks, when I was still predominantly a gym climber. I didn't yet know what climbing outdoors meant.
(Credit: Dierdre Wolownick)

With my mom on the summit of Tenaya Peak in Tuolumne Meadows, to celebrate her birthday. I look like I have a paunch, but that's only because of the afternoon updraft filling my shirt.
(Photo credit: Sean McCartney)

On top of Mount Whitney with my sister, Stasia, during *Sufferfest 1*. I soloed a route up the Keeler Needle while she scrambled up the Mountaineers Route, and we met on top. *(Credit: Cedar Wright)*

My first solo of the Rostrum. I climbed through this roped party and then ran into them on the bus later and got the photos. Note the torn shorts and random hand-me-down shirt—this was in the days before sponsorship. *(Credit: Honnold Collection)*

Soloing splitter finger cracks up high on Moonlight Buttress. Don't worry, this is easier than it looks. *(Credit: Sender Films)*

High on Half Dome, re-creating my free solo of the Regular Northwest Face. *(Credit: Jimmy Chin)*

Walking face-out across Thank God Ledge is surprisingly scary. Normally, walking across a ledge is trivial compared with actual rock climbing, but in this case it's quite an experience. *(Credit: Jimmy Chin)*

I remember almost nothing about this route except that it was fun and mellow. One of the few really nice cracks at Smith Rock. *(Credit: Ben Moon)*

Flipping through my old climbing journal while lounging in my van.
(Credit: Ben Moon)

Home life in the van in 2010. This was the second-generation interior, pretty rustic compared with the way it looks now.
(Credit: Ben Moon)

Leave two men alone shooting portraits in a house and pretty soon it devolves into seminude feats of strength. *(Credit: Ben Moon)*

Just fun crack climbing.
(Credit: Dawn Kish)

Taking it easy between climbs at Smith Rock.
(Credit: Dawn Kish)

Dynoing between crack systems while trying to free climb on our new route on Mount Kinabalu in Borneo. The mist below was a constant threat—it would rise up and engulf the wall, making everything too wet to climb.
(Credit: Jimmy Chin)

Mark Synnott and James Pearson were trying to climb the other side of this arch, and I became bored waiting, so I quested up the opposite pillar to try to beat them to the summit. But I had to downclimb after being turned around by bad rock and scary conditions. *(Credit: Jimmy Chin)*

Climbing on very soft sandstone high above Chad's Ennedi Desert. Adventure climbing at its finest. *(Credit: Jimmy Chin)*

ABOVE Normally a photographer shoots top down, hanging from a rope. In this case, Andrew Burr had to wait for me to get the rope up to the top, so he spent his time trying to create art while I climbed. Squamish has big ferns! *(Credit: Andrew Burr)*

BELOW My van, before I had cabinetry! Home sweet home. *(Credit: Andrew Burr)*

ABOVE Deep-water soloing in Oman. We would just stop wherever it looked interesting and put up new routes. Exploratory climbing at its best. And the snorkeling was even better than the climbing. *(Credit: Jimmy Chin)*

BELOW Soloing the Phoenix in Yosemite (5.13), with Cascade Creek raging below. This was one of my more intense solos, partly because you have to rappel in to get to the start. As soon as I started climbing, I was massively exposed and on difficult terrain. *(Credit: Sender Films)*

My first attempt at alpinism. Notice
how awkward and uncomfortable I look
compared to Freddie and Renan. Snowy
mountains are scary! *(Credit: Renan Ozturk)*

Near the summit of Mount Dickey,
approaching midnight in Alaska.
(Credit: Renan Ozturk)

Base camp below
Mount Dickey
on my first trip
to Alaska's Ruth
Gorge. It's hard to
tell how huge the
walls are, since
the glacier offers
no perspective, but
this face is almost
twice as big as the
biggest walls in
Yosemite. *(Credit:
Renan Ozturk)*

Soloing Separate Reality (5.11d). Though it's not really that hard, Separate Reality is a classic and historic route. I soloed it mostly to pay respect to all the people who'd done it before me. *(Credit: Jimmy Chin)*

Soloing one of the upper pitches of El Sendero Luminoso. Technical 12a face climbing. Good times! *(Credit: Renan Ozturk)*

The Fitz Traverse, with route and camps marked.
(Credit: Rolando Garibotti)

Our bivy on the first night of the Fitz Traverse, a little way past the summit of Aguja Mermoz. Tommy and I felt like this was the most scenic camping trip of our lives. The tent added some major comfort, since we were sharing a sleeping bag with no pad.
(Credit: Tommy Caldwell)

On the Fitz Traverse, it was hard to take photos of each other, since we were mostly climbing at the same time. But on the north pillar of Fitz Roy, I ended one block and Tommy took the lead, so we were right next to each other. (Credit: Alex Honnold)

Tommy rapping off the summit of Aguja Rafael, after we climbed Blood on the Tracks, a 12ish pitch. Everything felt hard. (Credit: Austin Siadak)

Mountaineering makes you manly! Or maybe just worked-looking. *(Credit: Austin Siadak)*

Sean "Stanley" Leary and I were heading back up to El Cap while climbing it three times in one day in 2010. Sean was the most motivated big-wall speed-climbing partner anyone could ask for. On easy terrain, he would practically run uphill. He was amazing. *(Credit: Tom Evans)*

That's me atop the Cobra during *Sufferfest 2*. Disconcertingly, the tower fell over not long after our trip. Soft sandstone is such an impermanent thing. *(Credit: Cedar Wright)*

Having learned nothing from our previous follies in the High Sierra, Cedar and I launch *Sufferfest 2* among the sandstone towers of the Southwest. *(Credit: Cedar Wright)*

CHAPTER **SIX**

THE SPEED RECORD

THE ONE-DAY ASCENT OF THE NOSE in 1975 by Jim Bridwell, John Long, and Billy Westbay dazzled the climbing world. Their time on the wall—a shade under fifteen hours—shaved an astounding twenty hours off the previous record, set just the year before.

It was inevitable that someone would show up and climb the Nose even faster than the trio of legendary Stonemasters. In 1979, a French ace, Thierry Renault, came to the Valley and surged up the route in under thirteen hours. His ascent was notable in view of the fact that most European climbers get shut down cold on their first visits to Yosemite, either because they're unused to severe crack climbing or because they're simply intimidated by the sheer, sweeping granite walls. Renault made so little fuss about his deed that the name of his climbing partner seems lost to history (the compendia of speed climbs simply cite "Thierry 'Turbo' Renault + other").

Five more years passed before Renault's time was bettered. Again, the new record was claimed by climbers from abroad. On the summer solstice in 1984, the Brit Duncan Critchley and the

Swiss Romain Vogler pulled off the ascent in the remarkable time of nine and a half hours.

Then along came Hans Florine.

An All-American pole vaulter in college, Florine started climbing in his native California at the age of nineteen and almost at once realized that his forte was speed. Early on, he won virtually every speed competition on artificial walls that he entered, including three gold medals in the X Games. It was logical that Florine would turn his attention to the Nose.

In 1990, at the age of twenty-five, Hans paired up with Steve Schneider to lop nearly an hour and a half off the Critchley-Vogler record. Their time on El Cap, from base to summit, was eight hours and six minutes. But the new record didn't last long, as Peter Croft and Dave Schultz cut the mark to 6:40.

As mentioned in previous chapters, Peter Croft was one of the climbers a young Alex Honnold most admired, because of the bar he set with his solo climbs. Alex's free solos of Astroman and the Rostrum in a single day in 2007 gained him his first fame in the Valley, since no one had dared to try to repeat Croft's blazing feat during the previous twenty years. Six years older than Florine, Croft was a creaky thirty-two when he set the new record on the Nose.

With that, the race was on. Times were now clocked to the minute, not the more casual "slightly under X number of hours." Unlike most of his peers, who tend to minimize the role that competitiveness plays in their lives, Florine has always unabashedly confessed to relishing head-to-head combat. In 1991, with Andres Puhvel, Florine took back the crown with a time of 6:01—only to have Croft return with Schultz and reduce the record to a mind-boggling 4:48.

It was always, however, a friendly competition, so it was apropos that the two masters paired up and went for an even faster time. In 1992, Florine and Croft set the mark at 4:22.

That record stood for the next nine years. Perhaps no one in the

Valley could imagine improving on such a stellar performance, or perhaps the speed record simply fell out of vogue. It was not until Dean Potter emerged on the scene that Croft and Florine saw their record challenged. In October 2001, climbing with Timmy O'Neill, Potter broke the four-hour barrier—just barely. Their time was officially noted as 3:59:35. For the first time, seconds, not minutes, were required to measure the race up the Nose. And for the first time, the rules were codified. The stopwatch started when the first climber left the triangular ledge at the bottom of pitch 1 on the route topo. It clicked off only when the second climber tagged the "official" tree about forty feet above the topmost anchors on the route.

By 2001, at the age of forty-three, Peter Croft was no longer keen to compete for the Nose speed record. Instead, he turned to the mountains, blithely putting up severe new technical, multipeak routes in the High Sierra. But Florine felt the burr under his saddle. In the same month as Potter's breakthrough, he teamed up with Jim Herson to knock exactly two minutes and eight seconds off Potter's mark. Florine was now thirty-seven years old, but apparently fitter than ever. Undeterred, Potter came back in November and, climbing with O'Neill again, blew the record out of the water with a time of 3:24:20.

Florine bided his time for eight months. In September 2002, paired with a new speed demon, the Japanese Yuji Hirayama, Florine trumped Potter's feat. The duo not only broke the three-hour barrier: their time of 2:48:55 bested Potter and O'Neill's mark by 34.5 minutes.

The race was now a pitched battle. Out of nowhere, it seemed, the German brothers Alex and Thomas Huber jumped into the fray. In October 2007, they lowered the mark to 2:48:30—a mere twenty-five-second improvement on the Florine-Hirayama watershed. Only four days later, the Hubers improved their own record by two minutes and forty-five seconds.

All this rivalry only served to wave a red flag in Florine's face. Pairing again with Hirayama, he improved on the Huber brothers in July 2008 with a time of 2:43:33. Three months later, the duo broke their own mark, lowering it to 2:37:05.

Hans Florine, then forty-four years old, had held the speed record on the Nose seven times, losing and regaining it five times, and capping his amazing run by trumping his own best time by more than six minutes. Had the ultimate limit been reached? Dean Potter didn't think so.

At this point, Sender Films decided to document the whole show. Their twenty-two-minute film *Race for the Nose*, appearing as part of the Reel Rock Tour in 2011, captured the outlandish characters of the leading competitors and covered the action in scintillating you-are-there footage.

I really liked Sender's Race for the Nose *when I first saw it in 2011. Besides all the great action footage, which vividly captured just how hairy simul-climbing against a stopwatch can get, the film pitted these two great climbers—Hans Florine and Dean Potter—against each other in a classic mano-a-mano duel. They have such different personalities that the contrast only enhanced the drama.*

Dean likes to insist that he's not competitive, that he climbs for the spiritual rewards of perfecting his craft. Whereas Hans just lays it out there. The film billboards one of his pronouncements: "I love competition and I'm blatant about it. If it's something that makes me climb better than before, if it pushes me to do my best, then I see it as a good thing."

It's to Sender's credit that they get Dean to admit that the challenge of Hans's speed records brings out the competitiveness in him that's just beneath the surface. "He was like this little dog humping my leg," Dean says of Hans, "and so it brought out the little dog in me." Classic Dean!

The film focuses on Dean's attempt with Sean Leary to break the record on June 11, 2010. By then, Hans and Yuji's mark of 2:37:05 had stood for a year and a half. Before launching on the Nose, Dean announced, "I think it's possible to break the record by a large amount." But when Sean, coming second, tagged the tree on top of El Cap, the stopwatch clicked off at exactly 2:36:45. They'd broken the record, but only by twenty seconds. That didn't dampen their wild celebration on top.

Dean and Sean had considered their first attempt only a practice run, so their time was impressive. But before they could push the route to their absolute limits, winter storms hit the Valley and shut down the climbing season.

Watching that film made me want to give the record my own best shot. And I thought it would be really cool if I could do it with the old master, Hans. At the end of my great season in the Valley in 2012—climbing the Triple with Tommy Caldwell, then climbing it solo—I was in such good shape that I thought I should go for the Nose. By then, Hans was forty-seven years old, but I knew that he always stayed in tremendous shape. And I knew that he'd love nothing better than to take the record back from Dean.

Hans is a super straight-up dude with everybody. Like the way he makes no bones about loving competition. To me, he epitomized the successful older climber. By 2012, he had a wife he loved and kids he loved, but the fire was still in his belly. He didn't hesitate to accept my invitation. He lives in the Bay Area, so he wouldn't be acclimated to Yosemite. He just came up and took on the challenge as a weekend warrior.

The one thing Sender may have overemphasized in Race for the Nose is the ruthlessness of the rivalry. All the guys who are interested in the speed record are friends of mine, and of each other. I even gave Sean some beta—route-finding advice—before he and Dean went up to break Hans and Yuji's record. Some climbers look askance at speed records—they even criticize us for (so they think) corrupting the purism of ascent. My answer is simple: I do it because it's so much fun.

The whole thing started, I suppose, with the cachet of "Nose-in-a-day," which has bloomed as the acronym NIAD. That's still a cherished goal for many climbers. Of course, the whole in-a-day thing is arbitrary. Twenty-four hours is an arbitrary measure. If it had taken me twenty-five hours to do the Triple Crown solo, I'd still have felt pretty good about it.

Going for the Nose speed record is simply a fun game. All this stuff is a game.

Hans and I started our stopwatch on June 17, 2012, the day before his forty-eighth birthday. And I'll have to say, we climbed the route about as efficiently as is possible. Our teamwork was perfect. The only glitch (if you can even call it that) came in the Stove Legs, on pitches 8 and 9, when Hans slowed down a little. When Hans tagged the tree at the finish line, we stopped the watch. Our time was 2:23:46. Pretty rad, we both thought. We'd knocked thirteen minutes off Dean and Sean's record. Hans was overjoyed. I was surprisingly pleased myself.

After the climb, as we were walking down the backside of El Cap, I asked Hans, "Hey, what happened there in the Stove Legs?" He said, "I was catching my breath." "What do you mean 'catching your breath'?" I needled him. "We were going for the speed record!"

It's now been more than three years since Hans and I broke the record and nobody has bettered our time. Of course, that's mainly because no one has tried. We'll see how long it takes for someone to get properly motivated to go after it.

All the same, someday I'd like to try to break the two-hour frontier. I think it's possible. It's a huge psychological barrier, like the sub-two-hour marathon, but sooner or later, I'm convinced, somebody will do it. If I'm right, that you can't climb any more efficiently than Hans and I did that day in June 2012, then the only way to do the Nose faster is to get fitter. The upper part of the route is really steep and pumpy. When you're climbing fast, your forearms get superpumped. The burn is intense. That's where fitter might mean faster.

That said, and as gratifying as setting the record was, I don't see speed climbing the Nose as the same kind of major accomplishment that the Triple solo was. It's on a much smaller scale, much lighter, and two and a half hours of any kind of climbing doesn't take the mental and physical stamina of linkups on big walls. Or of free soloing.

In the spring and early summer of 2012, I'd had my best season ever in Yosemite. I wasn't sure what I'd do next, though I had plenty of projects jotted down in "to-do" lists in my climbing and training journals. Would 2013 be another year of consolidation? Not in the ways I might have anticipated. . . .

• • • •

The revelation that had first come to me on our endless drive across the desert in Chad in 2010—that, compared to the men I saw spending all day turning mud into bricks, or the boys beating their donkeys to make them haul water faster, I had it pretty easy in life—had stayed with me. The eternal question was how that revelation should dictate the way I lived, especially after sponsorship made my life even easier.

One answer had to do with lifestyle. Ever since 2007, I'd lived out of the Ford Econoline van I had bought cheap as a five-year-old used car. By 2010, it was still pretty ghetto, but a friend of mine had installed industrial carpeting, side panels, finishing work, and sturdy insulation. I cooked my meals on a two-burner Coleman stove, slept in my sleeping bag with a bouldering crash pad for a mattress, and read by headlamp.

By 2012, I could easily have rented an apartment or a condo to live in, but I decided to stick with the van. One reason was that it gave me the ultimate freedom—a kind of traveling base camp as I drove from one crag to another, following the changing seasons. A permanent residence would have felt like an annoying anchor. Living in a van reflected my ideals of simplicity, frugality, and efficiency.

Instead of trading in the old Econoline for a spiffier model, I decided to refurbish the vehicle. Now it's a really well-crafted van, even though it's got 180,000 miles on it. Between climbing trips in 2013, I left my van with John Robinson, a seventy-year-old retired friend from Sacramento, who had built out his own van. He made all kinds of improvements to mine. In my kitchen area, there's a five-gallon water tank and, instead of the Coleman two-burner, a built-in range connected to propane tanks. All enclosed in nice, custom-made cabinets.

In back, where I sleep, I have to lie a little bit diagonal, because I'm slightly taller than the van is wide. I've put in a sliding curtain for privacy, or to keep the light out when I stop over in a well-lighted parking lot. Instead of the industrial carpet, I've now got a linoleum floor—Home Depot's finest.

What I call my foyer—where the side door opens into what used to be the back seats—is where I take my shoes off. It's also my bathroom, where I pee into a bottle.

Under the bed platform, John built a big sliding storage drawer where I keep all my climbing gear, just the right size for my bouldering crash pad. Side chambers for other stuff. I even haul around my baseball glove, in case somebody wants to play catch—it's a good way to limber up the shoulders.

Goal Zero, a solar company that sponsors me, was kind enough to install two sixty-watt panels on the roof of the van. They in turn power an inside battery, which I use to charge my phone and laptop—though it also powers the LED lights in the ceiling and the carbon-monoxide detector that John insisted on installing, saying, "If I'm going to do this, it's gotta be up to code!"

The Econoline is a full-size van, but I've got the smallest engine Ford offers—a 4.2-liter V6. It might not be a powerhouse, but it manages pretty well. And, to be honest, I don't know anything about cars. I think of mine more as a tiny house that moves.

There are of course drawbacks to living in a van. One is getting hassled by security guards. A few years ago, when I was climbing at Red Rocks, I went to sleep in the parking lot of Caesar's Palace in Las Vegas. I was awakened from a deep slumber by a loud knock on my window. I had no idea what hour it was. I opened the front door a crack to talk to the guy.

"You can't camp here like this," he said irately, as if I was doing him personal harm. "Oh, sorry," I said, "I thought it was all right since I was in the casino last night."

"You have to leave," he went on, with enough disdain in his voice for me to know what he thought of anyone who would dare to desecrate the sanctity of his Palace.

Groggy and irritated, I got in the driver's seat and took off. It certainly wasn't the first time I'd been harassed like that, nor would it be the last. But for some reason the exchange stuck with me, grating on my nerves. I think it was because I could tell how much he looked down on me, how disgusted he was that someone would consider living in a van. In retrospect, I wish I'd laid into him, asking how someone who spends forty hours a week riding around a parking structure on a neon bicycle has any right to look down on my lifestyle choices.

During that Vegas outing, I used the Whole Foods parking

lot for my Internet service. Their free Wi-Fi was strong enough
to cover the whole surrounding lot, so I would park as close as I
could to the building and settle into the back of my van for e-mail
sessions. In fact, I used the Whole Foods bathrooms at least once
a day as well, though I also bought a lot of their organic food, so I
felt like it all balanced out.

There's no convenient camping around Vegas (the Red Rocks
campground is ridiculously overpriced and underwhelming), so I
split my nights among various hotel parking lots, twenty-four-hour
grocery stores, and some of my friends' streets. Each venue was
well-lit and loud with the sound of traffic. Getting rousted by security and told to move along was just part of the game, and being in
a place like Vegas for a month or more really made me appreciate
moving on to Indian Creek in Utah—at the other end of the car-
camping spectrum.

Where Vegas is annoyingly bright and bustling, the Creek is
almost oppressively dark and sometimes lonely. The night sky is
full of stars and the only sounds are the animals (and occasionally drunk climbers). The word quiet doesn't really do justice to
the deep, peaceful calm that settles over the desert at night. The
camping is unregulated, so you basically just find an empty spot
that suits your fancy and you post up for as long as you'd like. I've
spent weeks at the Creek and marveled each day at how beautiful
the landscape is—it really never gets old.

But what did get old was having no showers, no cell service, and
no food. A lot of people, especially Americans, get all excited about
"going camping," about how cool it is to be out in nature with nothing around you. But I think that camping holds a special appeal
for those who don't do it routinely. I like showering, I like eating
out, I like being able to call my friends or check my e-mail. And as
beautiful or romantic a place like the Creek might be, I eventually
tire of camping—even if it's in a van.

The whole thing is a trade-off. But as of 2015, I still have no plans to buy or rent an apartment anywhere. In my newly spiffed-up van, solar panels and all, I'm pretty content.

. . . .

Making a lifestyle choice, of course, is merely a personal matter. What I'd taken away from Chad was a certain feeling that I had an obligation to do something for others, for those with fewer choices in life and fewer means to accomplish them. By 2012, thanks to sponsorship and commercials, I had more money than I needed to live comfortably. So I established the Honnold Foundation. Its motto is "Helping people live better, simply." The mission statement I posted on my new website read, "The Honnold Foundation seeks simple, sustainable ways to improve lives world-wide. Simplicity is the key; low-impact, better living is the goal."

Three years into its operation, the foundation is just getting started. But already we've funded projects that I'm excited about. One involves supporting SolarAid, a British nonprofit that runs a campaign to provide solar lamps to four countries in Africa—Kenya, Malawi, Tanzania, and Zambia—to replace the ubiquitous kerosene lanterns that are both costly and toxic. SolarAid's ultimate goal is to abolish the use of kerosene lanterns in Africa by the year 2020. Some folks might think that's a pie-in-the-sky dream, but it's sure worth trying to make it happen.

Another nonprofit we support, called Grid Alternatives, aims to provide solar energy for low-income housing in the United States. So far we've focused on California and Colorado. In the spring of 2014, we moved into the Kayenta region of the Navajo Reservation to start providing solar energy to traditional Navajo families, many of whom have spent their whole lives without electricity or even running water.

Some years ago, I went on what I called my God-hating kick,

as I read all the major manifestos arguing against the ideas of religion and an afterlife—Richard Dawkins, Sam Harris, Christopher Hitchens, and the like. During that period, I sometimes referred to myself as a "born-again atheist."

More recently, my reading kick has been focused on clean energy. I'm deeply worried about the future of the world in the face of climate change, the unbridled use of fossil fuels, and so on. It's this passion, as much as anything, that led to the idea of the Honnold Foundation.

CHAPTER **SEVEN**
ALASKA AND SENDERO

WHEN I INTERVIEWED ALEX in the fall of 2010 for *Outside* magazine, one thing he was adamant about was that he'd never take up mountaineering. Rock climbing was the be-all and end-all of his outdoor existence. "I read every issue of *Alpinist* cover-to-cover," he quipped, "but I flip right past all the pictures with snow in them."

Nonetheless, his natural curiosity had at times driven him to probe the literature of mountaineering. On an extended trip to England, he claimed, "I read all the classic British climbing books, but I could never remember them afterward. They were all the same, slightly different casts of characters, vaguely different mountains." Pressed on the issue, Alex waffled slightly. "Sure, I'd accept a free trip to Everest," he admitted. "Who wouldn't want to take a free hike to the top of the world?" And, "Maybe when I've got nothing left to live for, I'll climb real mountains. I can see myself at seventy-five, hunkered down in a cabin, going out on hikes, playing with my grandkids."

Thus it came as a complete surprise to learn in the spring of

2013 that Freddie Wilkinson and Renan Ozturk, two of the best young big-range mountaineers in the United States, had persuaded Alex to join them on an expedition to Alaska. Their objective was the Great Gorge of the Ruth Glacier, southeast of Denali—a stunning corridor of flowing ice surrounded by sheer granite walls soaring as much as 5,000 feet from base to summit.

In late May and early June, the trio assaulted three long routes on Mounts Barrille, Bradley, and Dickey. I took a keen interest in their progress, for the route they tackled on Dickey was first climbed way back in 1974 by Ed Ward, Galen Rowell, and me. Ours, in fact, was the first big-wall climb completed in the Great Gorge.

It was Renan who talked Alex into going on the trip. Longtime friends, both sponsored by The North Face, they had not only climbed together, but Renan had filmed some of Alex's free-soloing exploits. As Alex recalls, "I just thought it was a great opportunity to learn. I was single, had nothing to do myself, and two friends who are really good at what they do were willing to teach me something. I couldn't pass up the opportunity."

The previous year, in May 2012, Renan and Freddie had completed the Tooth Traverse, one of the greatest challenges in Alaska mountaineering, as they made a five-day enchainment of five savage spires linked by knife-sharp ridges, culminating in the Mooses Tooth, a dramatic monolith of granite and ice that stands like a sentinel guarding the northeast corner of the Great Gorge. The traverse required three bivouacs in wildly exposed positions and culminated in a nonstop thirty-eight-hour push on the Mooses Tooth itself.

Despite having fulfilled a dream that was four years in the making, Renan and Freddie were still drawn to the Ruth Gorge. For 2013, the men decided to explore the western side of the great glacial corridor. And instead of an all-out commitment like the Tooth Traverse, they set their sights on routes that had already been climbed by others, hoping to apply a pure, fast alpine style to test their own finely honed skills against those of their predecessors. "We decided to go after classics," says Freddie, "rather than one massive time-consuming project like the Traverse. Alex was our hired gun. We figured he could lead the long rock sections as efficiently as anybody we knew.

"We weren't trying to set record times per se. But we had a goal to try to do those routes in one long day each. Alex was coming off his big-wall Yosemite climbs where almost everything he did was within the confines of twenty-four hours."

At only 7,650 feet, Barrille is dwarfed by its neighbors, the Mooses Tooth at 10,335 feet and Mount Dickey at 9,545. Still, it has serious rock and ice routes on its eastern and southern faces that rise a full 2,500 feet from base to summit. In late May 2013, Freddie and Alex climbed the Cobra Pillar on Barrille. Nursing a cold, Renan sat this one out, as he had climbed the same line in 2009. The route had been put up by two legendary American alpinists, Jim Donini and Jack Tackle, in 1991. The first ascent had required a five-day push, of which two and a half days were spent marooned in a bivouac during a typical Alaskan storm. Now Alex and Freddie bombed up the route in a mere nineteen hours, in a relatively straightforward ascent.

Next the three men turned to a more serious, longer route on Mount Bradley, the impressive 9,104-foot peak just south of Dickey. The Pearl, a long, zigzagging, committed route on the mountain's south face, had been established in 1995 by a trio of Austrians—Helmut Neswadba, Arthur Wutscher, and Andi Orgler. The alpine-style ascent had taken five days to complete.

Making the Pearl's second ascent, Freddie, Renan, and Alex dispatched the route in forty hours round trip, including a complicated descent of the mountain via its southwest ridge. On the crux A3 aid pitch, Alex came into his own. According to Freddie, "There were some fixed copperheads on the pitch [nuts that are hammered into cracks, rather than slotted]. Alex stood on two or three of those pieces, which weren't very secure. We were halfway up the route, and because of the traversing down low, retreat would have been desperate. Alex was facing an ankle-breaker for sure if he came off."

Says Alex, "From the two fixed copperheads, the only pro on the whole long pitch, I made a few 11-plus or 12-minus free moves—which was very scary—until I got to a more continuous crack. So it was only a small section of hard free climbing, but it was actually pretty heroic. If I hadn't been psyched to free climb, we would have been pretty fucked. Rapping off from there would have been horrendous."

If Alex was indeed the hired gun on crux rock pitches in the Gorge, he was the acolyte on snow and ice. Says Freddie, "Renan and I gave him a pretty good intro to alpinism. He was a bit uncertain with the ice axe, and I don't think he ever got really comfortable wearing crampons." Alex concurs: "I didn't feel comfortable on skis, in crampons—even walking around camp felt wrong. I had no idea what I was doing."

In fact, growing up in balmy California, Alex had spent so little time in the snow that a glacier whose icy depths plunged invisibly 4,000 feet below his feet to bedrock was so novel that he treated it at times like a playhouse. According to Freddie, "At base camp we built a snow kitchen. Alex couldn't get enough of the shoveling, as he crafted benches, shelves, nooks and crannies. He has this frenetic need to exercise. Renan and I were happy to turn him loose on the shoveling. It was a real Tom Sawyer moment."

Yet Alex's manic impatience came to the fore during a five-day storm the men endured after Bradley. Freddie: "There was this typical Alaskan low-grade scud day after day. Alex was jumping out of his skin. He kept saying, 'What are we gonna do today?' He was like a golden retriever—we had to give him a job to do. So I told him, 'Today we're just going to lie in our sleeping bags. Your assign-

ment is to read a book.' He finally settled in. Read *The Prize*, this
nine-hundred-plus-page book by Daniel Yergin about oil and power,
cover-to-cover.

"We basically got along great," adds Freddie. "But during those
down days, Alex could become a bit of a whiner. He was always
comparing everything to Yosemite. 'God,' he'd say, 'I could be wearing shorts, sport climbing at Jailhouse.'" (Jailhouse Rock is one of
Alex's favorite crags, near Sonora, California.)

At last the weather cleared, and with only a couple of days left in
their Alaska "vacation," the trio set their eyes on the southeast face
of Mount Dickey.

Ed Ward, Galen Rowell, and I had been proud of the fact that in
1974 we got up the 5,000-foot wall in only three days, as we accomplished one of the first alpine-style ascents in the Alaska Range.
The second and third ascents of our route, three decades later, also
took parties of crack climbers three days. Alex, Renan, and Freddie
would be attempting the fourth ascent.

On Dickey, Renan led the first pillar, steep and beautiful climbing
on decent granite. Then he turned the lead over to the team's hired
gun on the giant headwall. The insidious potential trap posed by the
southeast face lies in the fact that about two-fifths of the way up the
wall, the granite turns into horrible "brown sugar." On our second
day of climbing in 1974, as the weather started to deteriorate, we
had pushed up into that potential blind alley, not at all sure that we
had enough hardware to rappel off should we run into a dead end.

Our crux came on the thirty-second pitch, where Galen, improvising wildly, drove a couple of baby angle pitons directly into the
crackless brown sugar, then drilled a dubious bolt into the junk—
the only bolt we placed on the route. It was obvious that there was
no way to scale the blank cliff above the bolt. Instead we lowered
Ed, who pendulumed to the right. Out of sight of our partner, Galen
and I waited anxiously. At last Ed yelled, "It goes!" He had found the

good granite again in a series of chimneys and cracks, the key to our upward escape.

On June 6, 2013, Alex surged up the wall in the lead, dispatching one difficulty after another, fixing the rope so that Renan and Freddie could follow on their ascenders. Alex climbed in rock shoes, while his partners followed in mountain boots. According to Freddie, after several hours Alex said, "I can't believe how easy this climbing is. But why am I so tired?"

Freddie reflects, "That crappy rock in the middle of the face would have freaked out most climbers. But Alex had plenty of experience with bad rock in places like Chad."

Both the second and third ascent parties had thought they were off-route in the middle of the face, until they ran into Galen's bolt. As we had done, they used it to lower one climber, who pendulumed to the right to reach the good chimney system. But Alex thought the bolt, which had now been in place for thirty-nine years, looked, as he put it, "pretty terrible." As he recounts, "Instead of rappelling, penduluming, and then aiding the chimney, I face climbed sideways across the rock and effectively skipped that pitch."

Alex, Freddie, and Renan took most of the aid out of our route. We had rated the climb 5.9 A3. They graded it 5.10c A0, meaning that what little aid they resorted to was as easy as aid climbing gets—little more than pulling on gear from time to time. Most of that 5.10 free climbing—child's play for Alex—would have been beyond our abilities in 1974.

According to Alex, "I led about a thirty-pitch block without really stopping. I kept thinking, *One more pitch, then I'll turn it over to Freddie*, but then I'd make an anchor, look up, and decide that I could climb at least one more pitch before I gave up the lead.

"Freddie led the last five hundred feet on scary mixed terrain. He was our ice ninja!"

The trio's elapsed time—nineteen hours—made a hash of our

three-day push in 1974. On the other hand, those three climbed Dickey on a perfect, windless, sunny day—the finest during the previous several weeks. In 1974, we had finished the climb in a raging storm, with snow lashed by a forty mph gale, and we were glad to have survived our ascent.

A few weeks after their climb, I sent Alex a congratulatory e-mail. His return message was a model of magnanimity. "Your route on Dickey was awesome," he wrote, "and I can only imagine how crazy it would have felt to set out up a wall that big so long ago. I come to walls like that having soloed bigger linkups in a day, but back then it must have been truly grand."

In a Q&A with his friend Jimmy Chin, Alex was asked what had been the most "eye-opening experience" during his Alaskan sojourn. "I learned tons of little things," Alex answered, "like how to put my crampons on and how to use my ice tool, but in a general sense it was still just climbing. I guess the thing that surprised me the most was how much shit—rock and snow and ice—is constantly falling down the faces. Alpine climbing is dangerous!"

Even after the expedition to the Ruth Gorge, Alex insisted that he had no intention of becoming a mountaineer. "Climbing a peak like Ama Dablam," he says, referring to a stunning 22,349-foot mountain rising above the Khumbu Valley near Mount Everest, "has absolutely no appeal to me." On the other hand, in his e-mail to me after Dickey, Alex confessed, "Anyway, I'm psyched to go back to the Ruth Gorge someday. Such massive walls. But I'm trying not to get too sucked into alpine climbing."

Toward the end of 2013, however, Alex turned his rabid attention to a climbing objective that stood at the polar opposite of big walls in Alaska. It was a route on a limestone cliff in the Mexican state of Nuevo León. By 2013, Cedar Wright and Alex had become close friends and frequent partners on the rope, even though Cedar was eleven years older. They had met by accident on El Capitan in

2006, before Alex had won the fame he garnered from his one-day free solos of Astroman and the Rostrum. Cedar remembers being impressed by the shy young climber who seemed to come into his own the moment he started up a cliff: *Who's this kid?* he wondered to himself.

The two were together on the trip to the Czech Republic that fueled Sender's seminal 2008 film *The Sharp End*. Later, after Alex got sponsored by The North Face, their bond intensified. "We hit it off," Cedar recalls. "We shared the same sardonic sense of humor." And Cedar detected the modesty beneath Alex's sometimes "aggro" exterior. "It's just that Alex can't understand why anybody would have trouble climbing anything," he says.

Cedar was developing a career as a filmmaker himself, just as Renan Ozturk was doing at the same time, so it was almost inevitable that the three would collaborate on a major project. It all came together on El Potrero Chico.

Before January 2014, except for *Moonlight Buttress, nearly all of my big free solos had been on granite walls in Yosemite. But I'd first climbed on El Potrero Chico—"The Little Corral"—in 2009 and immediately enjoyed the highly technical style demanded by its gray limestone. It may be the best crag in Mexico, and it's certainly the best known. The whole ambiance of the place is congenial. There's a website devoted to singing the praises of Potrero, which offers "a lifetime of well-bolted, multi-pitch sport routes with ratings from 5.7 to 5.14 and routes with up to 23 pitches. The climbs have very easy access with only a 5-minute walk from most campgrounds, eliminating any need for a car. The cost of living is very low and the friendly people wonderful." Sounds like tourist hype, but those words match my own experience there.*

Of all the routes on Potrero, the gem is a fifteen-pitch route that arrows right up the middle of the face, called El Sendero Luminoso—"The Shining Path." The first ascent was put up by Jeff Jackson, Kevin Gallagher, and Kurt Smith in 1992. Two years later, Jackson, Smith, and Pete Peacock freed the whole 1,750-foot climb. They rated it 5.12d. But the climb is quite sustained, eleven pitches of 5.12 and four of 5.11. Jeff is the editor of Rock *and* Ice, *and we've corresponded quite a bit over the years, including when I wrote for the magazine or its website.*

I first climbed Sendero in 2009, and I'd immediately fantasized about soloing it. But when I came back in the winter of 2013–14 to revisit the route, I realized that it would take a concentrated effort for me to feel comfortable on it. Sendero climbs a north-facing wall with a lot of vegetation, and since the climbing is sufficiently difficult to keep the crowds away, there's not enough traffic to keep the route buffed clean. Holds were full of dirt and plants, and even though I could climb around them or avoid the particularly prickly cactuses, it's hard to commit when in the back of your mind you're wondering if there's an easier way. Potrero also has a reputation for being chossy, but I think that's overrated. Yes, there are a lot of loose blocks on the wall, but you just have to avoid grabbing or standing on them. The smooth limestone texture of the wall is actually pretty nice.

Part of the appeal of Sendero for me lay in the technical complexity of the climbing. Potrero is made of slabby, gray, water-runnel limestone. It's full of small holds and solution pockets. Really subtle features. All the holds tend to face the wrong directions. You get into tricky body positions that require real precision. It's so stylish—such an old-school climb.

Of course limestone is more porous than granite. Holds just break off unexpectedly. It's less predictable than granite. There are holds that are sort of "glued" to the wall. You have to trust that the one time you hold it is not the time it rips off the mountain.

The plan that winter was for Cedar and Renan to come down to Mexico to make a short film if I decided to solo Sendero. Almost at once, however, I had my qualms about the project. Ever since my "epiphany" in Chad, I'd agonized over the environmental impact of my climbing. To fly the three of us down to Mexico—not to mention other crew members to operate automated drones to capture footage high on the wall—would be to leave a sizable carbon footprint. Could I really justify burning all that jet fuel and using pricey high-tech hardware just to capture my several hours of play on Portrero Chico? What if we got everybody down there, ready to film, and I chickened out because I decided I wasn't comfortable going up on the wall without a rope?

In my mind, our Newfoundland trip in 2011 was a classic example of waste. Both a waste of our time and a waste of natural resources. We all flew to Newfoundland, drove to Devil's Bay, and rented a boat to cruise around the fjords, and we didn't climb shit. We made a huge impact on the environment—for nothing.

There was no guarantee I'd be up for the free solo. I've had other projects I set my eye on—notably Romantic Warrior in the Needles of California, a nine-pitch 5.12b route on a steep granite crack system—that I rehearsed, planned, and then backed off. It was too hot that June, my shoes didn't feel quite right, I felt rushed by other engagements I'd committed to in the upcoming days, so I realized I wasn't ready for it. Actually, there are tons of solos that I haven't done! In such a situation, I have to pay attention to my feelings and my judgment, not to outside pressures. So there was a real possibility in January 2014 that I might be dragging Cedar and Renan and the other guys down to Potrero Chico for nothing.

Starting on January 9, Cedar and I spent four days (with a rest day when it rained) climbing, fixing, and cleaning the route, using ropes and belaying to get the moves down pat and grigris to hold us in place while we cleaned. To get all the dirt, twigs, grass, and shrubs out of the cracks, we scraped away with our climbing brushes. They're like toothbrushes with extra-stiff bristles. If we'd really been serious, we would have used something more heavy-duty, like a big scrubber.

Each day, we worked from sunrise to sunset. The more vegetation we pulled off the upper pitches, the more dirt rained down on the lower ones. The more big plants we removed from the route, the more the small ones stood out. Once we started, we couldn't stop until we saw a perfectly clean slab of limestone. Some of the plants were particularly tough to get out, adapted as they are to rugged conditions. For a week after I returned to the States, I had thorns growing out of my hands. But Jeff Jackson e-mailed me, "God smiles every time you uproot a lechuguilla."

Purists or nonclimbers might think that by removing natural vegetation from a cliff, you're altering or even trashing the landscape. I'll confess to faint qualms along those lines. Cedar and I knew that plants grow back quickly on Potrero, and that the wall would eventually revert to a hanging garden. I didn't worry much about our impact while we swung around plucking cactuses and ticking holds. I just felt a vague sense of unease that we were putting so much work into something that's supposed to be so pure and simple.

But at the end of the fourth day, as we rapped down a smooth, clean face, I couldn't help feeling a giddy excitement. At some point, a switch had flipped from "Maybe I'll solo it eventually" to "So psyched! Must solo immediately!" I have no idea what flipped that switch, though the climbing did look more inviting without the dirt and plants obscuring the holds. For whatever reason, I was ready, and I knew that I would solo the route the next morning, if the conditions allowed.

That's the strange paradox, for me at least, about free soloing. It's the waiting beforehand that's anxiety-producing. The vacillating over "Should I do this?" When I finally commit, the stress goes away. It's actually a big relief to go up there and do it.

January 14 dawned clear. I wasn't going to delay any longer. I wanted to go up on the route alone, which is sort of the point of soloing. I was seeking out a personal adventure, and the filmmakers knew that any intrusion would fundamentally alter the experience. Renan took up a position far out in the desert at the base so he could get a long shot. Cedar spent several hours guiding the drone pilots up to the summit of El Toro so they could meet me on top and film some summit footage.

I was and felt completely alone. I didn't know where the other guys were positioned or if they were even watching. I just went climbing, knowing that we could go back up on the route during the next few days to get all the filming done.

The high-tech gear was brought to Mexico by a Boulder-based firm called SkySight. The drone was a small octocopter, maybe half the size of a coffee table, with a super-expensive gimbal that held a RED camera steady. Between the high-quality drone and the top-of-the-line cinema camera, and the fact that the guys at SkySight are among the best in the industry, we were pretty sure we'd capture some amazing scenes. The drone was flown by a pilot using a big controller—a lot like a toy truck. The camera was operated by the pilot's brother. And they brought along their sister as an assistant to help carry gear and catch the craft on landing.

Renan was there shooting for Camp 4 Collective, which had been hired by The North Face to make a film of the ascent. Camp 4 owns a RED camera, so Renan had been shooting with it for years. And Renan had brought his girlfriend to be a camera assistant, so that brought the filming crew to a total of five people. And then Cedar and me as climbers.

The morning of the solo, nobody said much of anything, because they didn't want to influence me one way or another. Earlier, though, everybody had assured me that I should climb only what I felt comfortable with, and that they could shoot any other, easier route if I changed my mind. But it was hard not to feel a little pressure.

We'd rented a small casita sitting atop a hill above one of the many camping areas, which provided a glorious view of the whole area. That morning I opened my eyes lazily, gazing up from the pile of jackets I was using as a pillow through the worn, faded blinds to see the tops of the mountains just catching some morning sun. Despite the pressure, I'd slept well. I almost always sleep well, even before big solo climbs. From the sofa I used as a bed I could easily see Sendero weaving its way up the wall. There was no way of escaping. I followed my normal routine—cereal poured into the yogurt tub, news on my phone. But I lingered, trying to stay patient and let the morning humidity burn off. I focused artificially on my phone, using it to ignore the people around me with cameras and questions, but not really understanding what I read. The only thing that mattered was Sendero, just coming into the light.

Finally, I made the fifteen-minute stroll over to the base of the route, weaving through scrubby, prickly bushes and struggling up a loose scree slope. My light backpack made me feel buoyant as I scrambled up the hill. My shoes, chalk bag, energy bars, and water felt weightless compared to the 600 feet of rope and full rack that we'd been carrying the past few days.

One of my favorite aspects of soloing is the way that pain ceases to exist. The previous four long days of climbing and cleaning had worn out my fingers and toes, but now, as I pulled on the first few holds, I felt none of the soreness. Each edge seemed perfect and crisp, each fingerlock felt like an anchor. Foot jams that had been hideously painful the previous afternoon felt rock solid. Hold after hold, I worked my way up the wall, smoothly and perfectly.

What seemed to me to be the crux of the route came at the top of the second pitch, maybe 250 feet above the ground. The standard sequence involves opposing side pulls with small and slippery footholds, but I'd found a small two-finger pocket out to the side that felt slightly more secure. As I chalked up, I felt a little nervous. Or maybe just excited. Or maybe just my awareness was heightened. It's hard to untangle the various feelings, but I definitely felt alive. I knew that this was the only moment on the route where I'd have to try really hard. And that's exactly what I did, completing the sequence exactly as I needed.

Once I calmed down a little from overgripping, I knew I'd finish the route, even though there were still thirteen pitches to go.

A second crux comes on the fifth pitch, about 600 feet off the ground. The pitch ends in a huge ledge where you can stop and take a breather. On the crux sequence, I was connected to the wall by only a small, sharp limestone undercling above my head. Trusting a tiny smear for my left foot, I raised my right foot almost to my waist, and I levered off it to reach my left hand to a distant jug.

It was by no means the hardest climbing on the route, but the stark simplicity of the movement stayed with me long afterward. To me, that is soloing at its finest: to be nearly disconnected from the wall with the air all around. There's a certain purity to that kind of movement that can't be found with a rope and gear. But for all my love of simplicity, it's not always simple to get to those positions. Here on Sendero, everything came together—a perfect mixture of aesthetics and challenge, hard enough climbing to demand total concentration and commitment on a line of strength that goes straight up the biggest face on the massif.

From there to the top, I climbed easily, trusting my feet more with each step. I used new sequences on a few pitches, trusting myself to find the easiest way through the seemingly blank sea of limestone. On the midway ledge, I popped my shoes off, and again five pitches higher, just to let my toes relax after hundreds of feet of

technical slab climbing. But all in all, I'd found exactly the experience I was looking for: I was only a small dot on a vast, uncaring
wall, but for those two hours, I got to taste perfection.

· · · ·

We spent the next two days reclimbing and reshooting various
pitches of the route. It's anticlimactic to go back up a route to pose
all over it. The triumph of the actual achievement gets lost in what
follows. But as I slithered in and out of my harness on various
ledges, climbing different sections for the camera and clipping into
anchors in between, I tried to remind myself that I wouldn't have
the opportunity to climb a wall like this one without doing some
work, and at least I was having fun with my friends.

From the start of our trip, Cedar had wanted to try to redpoint
Sendero—lead it free but roped, with no falls. I owed it to my buddy
to be his belay partner on such an effort. The trouble was, we had
return flights booked for the following morning. So we set out on
the evening of January 16 to try to climb the route in the night.

The full moon rose as he started up the first pitch, casting a
pale glow across the whole wall. There's something eerily calm
about moonlight. I left my headlamp off, and I fed out slack in the
darkness, pondering the last week. Was it worth it? What had we
really done?

For the first five pitches, Cedar moved steadily up the wall,
the silence punctured only by the occasional "I'm off belay. Line's
fixed!"—my cue to start jugging as fast as I could up the rope he'd
tied to his anchor. That way, Cedar could conserve the energy he
otherwise would have wasted on belaying and rope management. I
tried to jug each pitch in four minutes flat.

It was at this point, however, that the ethical dilemma of my
little "project" started to nag at me. Traveling to places like Chad
has made me acutely mindful of my own impact on the world

around me. At first, I'd assumed that my carbon footprint would be much lower than that of the average American, because I lived in a van and didn't own many possessions. But as I read more about the issue, I realized that the amount of flying that I did still left me near the highest percentile of environmental impact. My next thought was to buy carbon offsets—until I researched them and discovered that they weren't the cure-all I was hoping for. Paying someone to plant trees in the First World seemed far less beneficial than providing clean energy in the developing world, though both could be considered to be offsetting carbon emissions. The first basically pays the rich while the second not only reduces fossil-fuel use but also improves standards of living by saving people money and reducing the health problems associated with burning things for fuel.

I've tried to approach environmentalism the same way I do my climbing: by setting small, concrete goals that build on each other. That was the idea behind starting the Honnold Foundation. I also worked on smaller projects, such as setting up my mom's house with solar panels and giving up meat in an effort to eat lower on the food chain. In some ways it might seem silly even to make the effort, since the environmental problems facing our world are so much bigger than any one person's actions. But some walls also seem so huge and impossible that it appears pointless to work toward them. The beauty of climbing has always been the reward of the process itself.

While Cedar struggled through the intricate slabs, I couldn't help wondering whether making a whole production out of climbing went against all the environmental principles I wanted to stand for. Could radio-controlled heli shots and minimalism really go together? Was it worth the impact of flying a whole crew down to Mexico for me to enjoy one three-hour climb? Or could I possibly use the climbing to do more good than harm? Might the platform I've gained through climbing be harnessed toward more useful things?

The problem with worrying too much is that it can be crip-

pling. Somehow, I thought, it must all come down to balance—
finding that line between minimizing impact but still maintaining
an acceptable quality of life. But who's to judge an acceptable life?
I don't even know what I truly require to be happy. Do I have to
be traveling all the time? Or soloing walls? The circle of Cedar's
headlamp drifted slowly away, leaving me alone in the moonlight
to swim with my questions.

Then, when we were halfway up the wall, a mariachi band
started playing loudly just down the road from the cliff, filling the
still desert night with the blaring sounds of horns and accordi-
ons. We couldn't help laughing. I told Cedar they were rooting for
him. The moon tracked across the sky as I jugged to the rhythm of
live music. At the belay, I pulled my hood closer against the cool
night air. The summit loomed hundreds of feet above, silhouetted
against the starry blackness. Though it seemed impossibly far off,
there was nothing to do but carry on. Cedar continued tiptoeing up
into the night, savoring the voyage.

THE CAMP 4 COLLECTIVE FILM that Renan Ozturk crafted
to feature Alex's solo of El Sendero Luminoso, a mere six minutes and twelve seconds long, is a minor masterpiece. If it lacks the
gonzo zaniness of the Sender Films celebrations of Alex's deeds, as
well as the humorous riffs in van or campground, it captures the
grace of Alex's movement on rock better than any previous footage
has. The camera work, zooming fluidly in and out, or floating gently
through space (thanks to the SkySight drones), paints a lyricism
that mirrors Alex's state of mind and body when he's doing what
he does best.

There are moments in the film that bring home the seriousness
of free soloing in novel ways, such as a bit when Cedar Wright, in

the days of cleaning the route before the climb, says, "It's kind of weird, helping your friend do something that you know could potentially lead to his death"—this, as the camera pans over the graveyard in the nearby town of Hidalgo. But the closing footage captures Alex standing on what look like "nothing" holds, his hands dangling free at his sides, as a slow grin takes over his face.

Shortly after the climb, Mary Anne Potts of *National Geographic Adventure Online* interviewed Alex. She asked, "Why did you smile at that moment on the wall?"

Alex's characteristic answer: "I have no idea since I haven't seen the film, but I'd assume because I was happy." To underline the point, he appended a happy face.

Indeed, in the makeshift register on the summit of El Toro, with a pencil stub Alex scribbled a note that a later visitor photographed. It read:

> 1/14/14
> Solo!!
> In two hours
> Alex Honnold
> Great day out!!

(Two hours on the fifteen-pitch climb, another hour to scramble to the summit of El Toro.)

The Camp 4 film closes with the bald statement: "It could be the most difficult rope-less climb in history." Almost two years later, no one has come forth to dispute that claim—except Alex. In outtakes filmed by Renan just after the ascent, he insisted, "It's not like this is the physical limit of my climbing. Not like the hardest thing I could do. It was well within my comfort zone." ("No Big Deal" Honnold at his deadpan best!)

Others weighed in less equivocally. On Supertopo.com, post-

ers expressed their awe. Wrote one, "The dude is so scary good.
. . . All you can do is shake your head in wonderment and amaze-
ment." Another: "Compartmentalizing fear is a very real thing, and
he excels at it. Or is he just so good that he's not afraid?" Yet another,
tongue in cheek: "I'd be way more impressed if he was human."

Jeff Jackson, editor of *Rock and Ice* and the author of the first
(roped) free ascent of El Sendero Luminoso in 1994, editorialized,
"What do I think? Well, honestly, I try not to think about it. . . . The
Sendero free solo is a different realm entirely—so bad it makes me
wonder if Honnold will ever get another visit from Santa."

Less ironically, Jackson—one of the strongest rock climbers of
his generation—analyzed the feat by comparing it to his own experience on the route. "To my knowledge," he wrote,

no one has ever soloed a wall with such sustained technical
climbing—11 pitches rated 5.12a or harder. The pitches are long
(the first five are 50 meters or longer) and unrelieved by big features where you can chill and shake out your feet. The wall is a
slab, mostly just under vertical, and if you've ever climbed a difficult
slab you know how mentally trying that kind of climbing can be. To
me, climbing a 5.12 slab is a little like pulling a rabbit out of a top
hat. There are elements of magic at work. Though it has been 20
years since I climbed the line, I clearly remember the feeling of getting away with something when I redpointed [climbed free without
falling] the second pitch. I skated through on updraft, sticky rubber
and whispered petitions to demons. . . .

And Honnold soloed that pitch! And all the others! Shit me! How
is that even possible?

Alex was not about to rest on his laurels. Less than a month after
his Mexican triumph, he was off to a part of the world he had never
visited, to try a climb of the sort he'd never before attempted.

CHAPTER **EIGHT**
FITZ

The Fitz Traverse was Tommy Caldwell's idea. As soon as he mentioned it, I said, "That sounds rad! Let's do it!" I was on board, even though I'd never been to Patagonia. I didn't even know anything about Patagonia.

Though it stands only 11,168 feet above sea level, Fitz Roy is the tallest peak in a tight cluster of amazing granite spires in southern Patagonia, on the border between Chile and Argentina. It's named after Robert Fitzroy, the captain of the Beagle on the famous 1830s voyage that gave Charles Darwin his first inklings about the theory of evolution. The first ascent, by the great French mountaineers Lionel Terray and Guido Magnone in 1952, may have been the most technical big-range climb performed up to that date anywhere in the world.

That cluster of peaks, which also includes Cerro Torre, Torre Egger, Aguja Poincenot, and many other agujas (Spanish for "needles"), probably comprises the ultimate collection anywhere on earth of steep, soaring, and breathtakingly beautiful mountains. The granite is shockingly good—as good as Yosemite—but Patagonia is notorious for bad weather, for shrieking winds that don't let up for weeks, and for humongous mushrooms of rime ice plating nearly vertical slabs and cracks.

Tommy first climbed in Patagonia in 2006. Even though most of his prior experience had been on rock, he put up some formidable lines that season. As mentioned in chapter five, Tommy, with Topher Donahue and Erik Roed, freed the Línea de Eleganza on Fitz Roy. Tommy and Topher also tried another massive route, Royal Flush, on the east face of Fitz Roy. The peak was pissing wet that February, and other climbers gave up on the climb, declaring it hopeless, but Tommy went up there in the same conditions and damn near freed the route onsight (on his first time on the route) before he and Topher had to back off.

By 2014, Fitz Roy had really gotten under Tommy's skin—so much so that the year before, when his wife, Becca, gave birth to a boy, they named him Fitz.

Though a formidable peak in its own right, Fitz Roy doesn't stand alone. It's the centerpiece of a chain of seven connected towers, starting on the north with the Aguja Guillaumet and ending on the south with the Aguja de l'S. The obvious challenge was to connect them all in a single continuous ridge climb—the Fitz Traverse.

In 2008, Freddie Wilkinson, who would be my partner five years later in the Ruth Gorge, and Dana Drummond completed the first half of the traverse, linking Guillaumet, Mermoz, Val Biois, and Fitz Roy, but then rapping off Fitz Roy and hiking out. They called their half-traverse the Care Bear Traverse, because they were stuck in the clouds so much of the time that they started joking with each other, "I bet all those other climbers are thinking, 'Those stupid Americans are up in the clouds!'" (In the children's cartoon series Care Bears, the ursine heroes live in lairs among the clouds.)

Freddie and Dana took three days for the traverse, with two exposed bivouacs. The Care Bear was repeated numerous times after 2008, but nobody had gotten beyond Fitz Roy. *The problem for all those teams was that because the second guy did so much jugging, by the time they got up Fitz Roy their ropes were pretty core-shot from rubbing against the rock.*

Tommy and I arrived in El Chaltén, the gateway town to climbing in the Fitz Roy region, on February 1, 2014. For the first nine days, the weather on the peaks was horrendous, so we climbed down low, bouldering and doing sport climbs on small crags. There's a ton of good climbing all around El Chaltén. Sweet! I thought. I'm gonna get strong! But I also thought, Wow, these peaks are so intimidating, I'm not sure I'd really mind if the weather never gets good.

We climbed every day, and ate out every night in El Chaltén. It was a pretty nice lifestyle.

C ALDWELL WOULD LATER WRITE about the Patagonia adventure for *Alpinist* in the winter 2014 issue. In his thoughtful piece, he talked about how much harder it was to climb with all-out commitment once he had become a father. "I'd had this Romantic idea," he wrote, "of pulling my family into my life of constant travel. So they followed me from Colorado to Argentina. Then, after two blissful weeks together in El Chaltén, the wind had calmed, and I'd packed."

Saying good-bye to Becca as he headed for the Fitz Traverse, Tommy minimized the danger. "Don't worry, baby, we'll be careful," he told her. "It's just a rock climb."

But privately, "I remembered that I wanted nothing more than to live to be an old man."

In the same essay, Tommy recalled meeting up with Alex in the Valley in the spring of 2012 and being taken aback by his nonchalance. "Anyone could daisy-solo the Regular Route of Half Dome," Alex claimed. "It's not that big of a deal. . . . You know you're not going to fall on 5.11."

Drawn to Alex by his skill and amiability, Tommy puzzled over his friend's almost blasé attitude about risk.

How could Alex talk about his climbs in such a cavalier way? . . .
[H]e described free solos of routes like the Regular Northwest Face
of Half Dome as if they were nothing more than particularly scenic
hikes. His conversation never drifted to places of death, love or
even innate beauty. *It's as if he thinks everything is either badass or
boring,* I thought. *That's probably part of the reason he is so good
at what he does.* I found Alex's apparent indifference toward risk
both exciting and terrifying. In an age of technology, he reminded
me of a lost instinct. A hunter, a warrior.

Whatever Tommy's doubts, he soon realized that he and Alex made a superb two-man team. On their Triple Crown linkup in 2012, in the middle of the night on Freerider on El Cap, Alex had been deeply impressed by Tommy's stemming a pitch in the dark that he normally would have liebacked. But Tommy was equally impressed by Alex's nerve and aplomb.

He rarely stopped to place gear, only a few pieces per pitch. Somehow, that boldness, that confidence that he wouldn't fall, was
contagious. . . .

Tied to the upper end of the rope, Alex was simul-climbing out
of sight and earshot. Above me, the cord arched past a dark offwidth—clipped to nothing. My arms quivered with fatigue; my head
pounded with dehydration. I hoped to God that he had some gear
in. Best not to think too much about it.

Even while they simul-climbed at a nearly perfect level together, Tommy and Alex engaged in a friendly debate about free soloing, with Tommy voicing his doubts. As Tommy would later comment, "Alex is as solid as anybody I've ever met on technical rock. But I worry about him. I've never tried to talk him out of free soloing—I just express my doubts. But he'll turn around and try to talk me *into* free soloing.

"We climbed Velvet Tongue at Red Rocks together, roped. Leading the 5.12+ crux, Alex slipped. But he hung on by one finger. Anybody else would have fallen off. I said, 'Wow, that was impressive!' But of course I was thinking, *What if he were soloing when that happened?*"

In the *Alpinist* piece, Caldwell explains how completing the Triple Crown with Alex gave him the idea for teaming up to attempt the Fitz Traverse. On the summit of Half Dome, after climbing some eighty pitches in twenty-one hours,

> I'd expected the trifecta to be a test of human will and endurance. I'd wanted to see that place of survival again, where we're reminded that human capabilities are nearly limitless and that our world still contains mysteries. But Alex was just too good. The big walls seemed to shrink to only half their size. . . . I wondered what we would be able to climb if we took these techniques to Patagonia, where the big storms and bigger mountains made fast and light climbing a necessity—rather than merely a cool trick.

When the weather finally cleared on February 12, with a forecast of a good window during the next few days, Tommy and I headed up. The big advantage we thought we had over previous parties that had tried the Fitz Traverse was that instead of having the second jug every pitch, we'd simul-climb almost everything. That ought to mean less wear and tear on our rope.

Just as we had on the Triple in Yosemite, we each led huge blocks at a time, upwards of 800 feet. Part of what makes climbing with Tommy so great is that we can lead interchangeably, though on this traverse he would get all the ice and mixed pitches, since he had vastly more experience with that terrain. We got up the first tower, Aguja Guillaumet, in only two very long pitches, taking a mere two and a half hours to climb the thousand feet of the Brenner-Moschioni route.

It turns out that Rolo—Rolando Garibotti—and Colin Haley were trying the Fitz Traverse at the same time we were. Rolo's the man when it comes to Patagonia—not only its tireless chronicler, but the guy who's put up more routes on more different peaks than anyone else. He's also become a kind of steward of the range, improving trails and assembling route guides. We met up with that pair on the summit of Guillaumet, since they'd climbed a different route. Rolo had had hip surgery the previous year, and now his hip was really bothering him, so, reluctantly, they abandoned their effort. Rolo was kind enough to lend me his aluminum strap-on crampons, which would turn out to be extremely helpful for the traverse.

We went really light, figuring speed would mean safety. Our rack was seventeen cams, a handful of nuts, and fourteen slings. No pitons. We were counting on finding fixed anchors and even fixed gear along the way, to supplement the pro we'd place as we led. The real question mark was whether we could find the rappel anchors left by other parties, so we could rap most of the big descents from each tower as we moved along the ridgeline.

We had one sixty-meter climbing rope, and a skinny eighty-meter tag line—a rope to use not for leading but for rappels. By tying the tag line and the lead rope together end to end, and feeding it through the anchor sling, we could make a rappel on the doubled rope as long as sixty meters, then pull the ropes down to use on the next rappel. For the ice, only one ice screw and a single ice tool—a Black Diamond Cobra, a short metal axe with a curved shaft and a sharp, notched pick.

We did most of the climbing in approach shoes, or tennies, as we call them. Rock shoes only for the hardest pitches. No mountain boots. We strapped our crampons onto our tennies, which doesn't make for the most stable configuration, because the soles and edges of the shoes are too soft and flexible.

One sleeping bag between us, and one big puffy (down jacket). A stove and three gas canisters. We originally planned not to bring a tent, but on one of our "training" days during the bad weather, we'd spent the night in our Black Diamond First Light tent and realized how comfortable it was. It's a pretty amazing shelter, because it weighs only one pound. At the last minute, we decided to take it. It turned out to be a godsend.

We were determined to go light enough that all our gear, stove, fuel, and food could fit into one fifteen-pound pack (for the leader) and one twenty-five-pound pack (for the second). For a multiday alpine traverse, that's pretty frickin' light!

Afterward, some clueless journalist asked us if we'd had a film crew along. As if! But Tommy had been given a very light camera, so we tried to take video clips of each other as we moved along the traverse—footage that might eventually be spliced together into a film documenting the climb. We also had iPhones to shoot photos with. Actually, my iPhone was one of my most important pieces of gear, because I had about sixty topos of the various routes on the various towers loaded onto it.

From the summit of Guillaumet, we ridge-traversed over to the Aguja Mermoz, topping out at 5:00 p.m. Four hours later, we set

up the tent right on the crest of the ridge and settled in for our
first night's bivouac. I got the puffy that night, and slept nice and
warm. It was only a few days later that Tommy confessed that he'd
basically shivered through the night. In fact, I hogged the puffy for
three nights, thinking that as a suburban California boy I needed
it more than a Colorado hardman did. At last, Tommy's reluctant
admission of how cold he was made me stop being selfish and give
him the puffy.

We got off at 8:30 a.m. on February 13. It took a long, long day
to climb over the Aguja Val Biois and up the Goretta Pillar via the
Casarotto route. There we found some of the finest rock climbing
on the whole traverse, with free moves up to 5.11d. That stretch,
which I led, was one of only a few passages on the whole traverse
where we switched to rock shoes. We French freed whenever we
could, either grabbing and pulling on fixed gear or popping in a
cam or nut and pulling on that. Still, we did very little aid on the
whole traverse, nothing that we'd rate harder than A1.

It wasn't until 7:45 p.m. that we stood at the base of the final
headwall on the north pillar of Fitz Roy itself. We were pretty darn
tired after more than eleven continuous hours of climbing, but this
was no place for a bivouac, so we decided to try to get up the headwall and camp on the summit. We also thought that the colder
snow conditions of evening would be safer than waiting till morning, when sun on the wall might send all kinds of stuff falling down
on us.

We could see at once that there was way more ice and snow
on that headwall than we'd expected, thanks to one of the wettest
summers in recent years. It was Tommy's turn to lead. As he forged
his way up into that mess of ice, snow, and rock, we faced what
would turn out to be the crux of the whole traverse. And here the
climbing got really scary.

. . . .

Crusted up with rime ice, that headwall would have been tough
enough to lead with a pair of ice tools, a good supply of screws, and
crampons firmly strapped onto mountain boots. For Tommy, with
only the one screw and the Cobra as his sole tool, and crampons
wobbling on his tennies, it was a nightmare. As he worked his way
up into the rime, he uncharacteristically shouted down, "I don't
know about this."

I tried to encourage him. "Dude, you got this," I shouted up.
"You're a total boss." But I had my own doubts and fears.

A waterfall was springing out of the ice, as Tommy put it, "from
a hole in the mountain that resemble[d] the mouth of a dragon."
He later captured that incredibly dicey lead in his Alpinist piece:

> I let the pick of my single axe pierce the sheet of flowing water and
> strike the new-formed ice beneath. The point glides around for a
> moment and then sticks in a small slot. I have to move now. In
> another thirty minutes, that cascade will freeze and coat everything
> in verglas. Our few cams will skitter, useless, out of the cracks, and
> the aluminum crampons strapped to our tennis shoes will be more
> like skates. My hand trembles. . . .
>
> I enter the waterfall, and I gasp as the cold flow seeps into
> every conceivable opening. I slot my single tool in a fissure, pull up
> and place a nut. . . . I look down: a large, dry ledge extends like an
> island below me. A growing chill reminds me that it's already too
> late to retreat. The only option, now, is to keep moving. I'd wanted
> us to have an adventure, but this is a bit too much.

For the next half hour, Tommy flailed around, as he described
it, "like a hooked fish in a rapid." Finally he leaned off his tool
placement far to the side and got a tiny cam partly slotted in a

crack. He wasn't sure it would hold, but he grabbed it with both hands and swung over. Soaked to the skin, he was shivering, on the verge of hypothermia, but at last he was on dry rock.

The sun had set a while before. Tommy switched on his headlamp and aided up the crack. At last he took off his crampons and free climbed beyond. As he later wrote,

> Coarse rock grates my skin. Blood splatters on stone. My clothes freeze. With each move, ice cracks off my jacket and chimes down the wall. The rope becomes as stiff as a steel cable. I climb faster, trying to create more body heat. . . . Occasionally, my only option is to chop through the rime that blocks our passage. Debris showers on Alex's head. Large chunks hit his back and shoulders with a guttural thud.
>
> "Are you OK?" I shout down.
>
> "Yeah, man, you're doing great," Alex says, but the words sound forced.

All this time, I was wearing both of our jackets, the big puffy in addition to Tommy's light puffy. He was leading in just his hoodie and hardshell. It was amazing because after he got soaked, he climbed a lot farther, then eventually dried out and got warm again. Since I was doing nothing but belay for forty-five minutes at a stretch, then jugging for fifteen minutes, I was getting kind of chilly. It was impressive that Tommy could keep it together in such cold temps. Total hardman.

Finally the angle of the headwall relented. But now, in the dark, Tommy led a 600-foot pitch of snow and mixed steps. You're just scrambling, except that it was really snowy. Since we only had the one ice tool, he was leading with it, which meant that I wound up simul-climbing in strap-on crampons with no tool. Since the rope just disappeared into the night and I didn't know if he'd gotten in any pro, I was seconding with only Tommy's pick marks to show me the route. And just generally clawing at the mountain with my hands. It was scary.

We didn't get near the summit until 2:00 a.m. Just below the top, we found a nook shaped by a cornice that gave us a lee space to set up our tent. "What a day!" said Tommy.

We got ourselves inside the tent and shared our single sleeping bag. Once again, since I had the puffy, Tommy shivered through the night without complaining.

I'll have to admit that, on that headwall, I was way outside my comfort zone. That was one of my hardest days of climbing ever.

After only three hours of fitful sleep, we packed up camp and hiked to the summit of Fitz Roy. We didn't spend long there, shooting a few photos, still dog-tired. But from here on, we were pushing beyond the Care Bear Traverse that Freddie Wilkinson and Dana Drummond had established in 2008.

To get off Fitz Roy and down to the col between it and the Aguja Kakito, we had to make twenty rappels down the Franco-Argentine route. The route was like a waterfall. Three days of sunny weather on a south-facing wall had melted everything in sight. The ropes were like sponges and we got massively wet—not that that was a big problem, since it was sunny and nice out. An acquaintance of ours, Whit Margo, had just successfully guided a client up one of the ice routes on the other side of Fitz, and we ran into him near the summit. He gave us good beta for how to find the rap anchors, which was really helpful. But then, as we were rapping the face, his client's ice axe came tomahawking past us at about a million miles an hour. He'd accidentally dropped it and it went the whole distance down the wall. It was kind of a weird encounter.

From the col between Fitz Roy and Kakito onward, though,

we were in largely uncharted terrain. We managed to weave our way over and around the various spiky summits of Kakito. But it was 6:00 p.m. before we stood at the base of the north face of Aguja Poincenot. Here we faced our second major rock climb, as we started up the route pioneered by Dean Potter and Steph Davis in 2001. It's a serious, 1,000-foot route with some bad rock and poor protection on a few pitches. Dean and Steph rated it 5.11d A1.

Our three days of nonstop climbing were starting to take their toll. The skin on Tommy's fingers was starting to be really painful, it was rubbed so raw. On Poincenot, I led the whole wall, but instead of simul-climbing, Tommy jugged up second to save his fingers. I short-fixed—tying off the middle of the rope to an anchor so he could jug while I soloed on—as often as I could to make it less arduous for him.

For one of the few times on the traverse, I switched to rock shoes. Then I managed to lead the whole thousand feet in only three and a quarter hours. There was only one pitch of truly bad rock, up at the top, but it was easy. And there was some semi-unprotected face climbing at the bottom that was spicy. But basically the route followed nice splitter cracks and I just charged along. I really felt like I was at home in the Valley. Really comfortable climbing.

Wasted as we were on the summit of Poincenot, we were still getting along great and climbing as efficiently as we knew how to. Throughout the traverse, we'd found time to take short breaks as we shot video clips on Tommy's camera. For voice-over, we added commentary about the whole undertaking. At one point, for instance, Tommy said, "This has gotta be the most scenic thing in the universe." On the summit of Fitz Roy, I'd seen other climbers maybe five hundred feet below us on a different route, and I couldn't help blurting out, "There are humans down there! We're going to go down and hug them!" Now, with the camera rolling, Tommy said, "Tell us where we are." I dutifully answered, "We're on the summit of Poincenot!" Corny, maybe, but who knows what a good film editor could do with that stuff.

We pitched our tent again just below the summit of Poincenot on the south side and managed to get another few hours of sleep. That night, Tommy tried to build a little tent platform out of rocks so we'd have something level to sleep on while I cooked dinner. He finally gave up about halfway through because he couldn't make it work. The ledge we were on was just too rocky and misshapen. So we wound up sleeping with our legs hanging over this big drop and a bunch of rocks sticking into our backs. There was always a junk show inside the tent. But we slept well enough. Fatigue does wonders. Still, I remember that bivy as the worst of the traverse.

By now we looked pretty haggard. We weren't eating nearly enough food to match the calories we burned, and our meal breaks were pretty on-the-run. I remember at one point both of us eating polenta with Tommy's broken sunglasses because we couldn't find our spoon. We were able to stay hydrated, however, by using straws we'd brought along to suck the standing water out of little huecos (natural pockets) in the rock. Or we'd eat snow while we were belaying.

By now, our gear and clothing were in tatters. Our shoes were falling apart, and our tent floor was full of little holes from pitching it on uneven rocks. Our pants had rips and tears in them. We'd managed to burn a hole in our sleeping bag. Our packs were trashed from dragging them through chimneys. Somewhere along the way, Tommy dropped one of his climbing shoes. We didn't even see it disappear into the abyss—it just suddenly went missing. On the Fitz Traverse, you could say that we product-tested a whole line of equipment.

Getting down the 3,000-foot south face of Poincenot proved to be the second crux of the whole traverse. That wall isn't climbed very often, but we absolutely had to find the fixed anchors left by other parties to continue our traverse. If we couldn't find those anchors, we'd easily use up our rack—and then some—making anchors of our own. And then, if we could get down, we'd have to abort and hike out. It's a scary business to rappel blind down a wall you've never seen before, looking for those fugitive pitons. I'd get fifty-five meters down and start thinking, Boy, I hope I find an anchor! We downclimbed as much as we could, but we had to rap most of the way. At one point, Tommy just picked up a stone and wedged it into a four-inch crack for an anchor. I said, "Wow. Did you ever do that before?" Tommy reassured me: "It's bomber."

In the end, we never got off-route. We pretty much nailed that descent.

By now, we were sort of flying on autopilot. Tommy described our state well in Alpinist:

> At times, a kind of mutual delirium builds like the electric charge of a thunderstorm. Chemicals release from our brains: dopamine, norepinephrine, endorphins. Our focus narrows and intensifies. More and more, we appear to think as one. A sixth sense seems to warn us of each loose block or hidden patch of black ice. . . . Each footstep is sure and precise. The absurdity of our situation makes us giddy.

We were beginning to think we could really pull off the traverse. There were only three towers to go, none as tall or as serious as Poincenot. We tackled the Piola-Anker route on Aguja Rafael Juárez. It's another thousand feet, rated by the 1989 first-ascent party 5.11a A1, but the rock is mostly good. I led in rock shoes, while Tommy alternately jugged or simul-climbed. Near the top of the route, though, I ran into a 150-foot-long 5.10b crack that took only number 4 cams. One edge of the crack was coated with ice. I didn't have a number 4 cam on my rack, so I kept pushing a number 3 in front of me and pulling on it. Because it was too small, it was tipped out, with the plates barely catching the edges of the crack. It would never have held a fall, but at least it helped with the climbing. That just goes to show that in an international arena like Patagonia, you never know what the ratings are going to wind up meaning.

Even so, we got up the Piola-Anker in two long pitches, taking only two and three-quarters hours. A little more than two hours later, we'd traversed the sharp ridge and climbed two longish pitches to the summit of Aguja Saint-Exupéry.

By now, though, our climbing rope was shredding, thanks to the countless abrasions we'd subjected it to as it rubbed against the gritty granite. One section was so badly damaged that we finally had to cut it, leaving us with only thirty-eight meters of usable rope. The other twenty-two meters we carried with us to cut into smaller pieces for slings for our rap anchors. What this meant, however, was that we could make only pitifully short rappels with our doubled remnant of rope—a maximum of nineteen meters. If it hadn't been so windy, we could have used our eighty-meter tag line to make longer rappels. We tried to use it, but it got so tangled up that it drove us insane trying to sort out the snarls. So we coiled it up, stuck it in a pack, and just resorted to shorter but safer raps on our thirty-eight meters of good lead rope.

Tommy would head down first, get to a stance, and yell, "I'm off!" I'd say, "I know, I can see you right below me"—scarcely sixty feet from my own stance. On a bunch of the gear anchors that we constructed, after Tommy rapped I would remove one of the pieces just to save gear. So I'd rappel off a single cam or nut, which can be a bit risky. (If it pops loose, you're dead.) I did that a few times in random places. It was all about preserving the rack for as long as possible.

On the ridge between Rafael Juárez and Saint-Exupéry, we were simul-climbing with the twenty-two-meter section of our lead line. (We were trying to save the longer part for climbing later, and twenty-two meters is long enough for ridge climbing.) In the lead, I got up to a little tower that dropped off maybe eighteen feet. No place to get in any pro. So I told Tommy to hang back a bit, and I climbed over the tower and rappelled off the other side, using his body weight as my anchor. Then, when he got to the tower, he just looped the rope around a little horn on top and rapped off the other end. So we were each tied into one end of the rope, rapping off each other's body weight. There was no actual anchor, just a little natural horn that the rope ran behind. When we were done, we just flicked the rope loose and it fell down.

It was a really weird configuration. We did all kinds of improvising like that. Which is what made things go fast.

The rappel off the south side of Saint-Exupéry is down a major wall. But here we were in luck. A few years earlier, there'd been a serious accident on this wall, so it was covered with trash from the massive rescue effort. Anchors, fixed ropes, junk all over the place. It seemed as though it took us an endless number of nineteen-meter rappels, and we were so tired it felt like a nightmare, but we got down it.

It was late evening. In the col below the last tower, the Aguja de l'S, we pitched our fourth camp. This time Tommy finally got the puffy, so he was warm. I did okay myself, since we were at a relatively low altitude. That night, we got a solid six hours of sleep. But the alarming fact was that we didn't feel at all recovered in the morning. By this point, we were just crushed.

On the fifth day, we got really blasted by the famous Patagonian winds, blowing out of the west, at our backs. It was so gusty as we pushed up the Aguja de l'S that we had to wait and time our bursts of climbing around the gusts. The wind was threatening to blow us off our feet. But we got over the Aguja de l'S and down to the glacier by 10:00 a.m. The relief was tremendous. All we had to do now was hike out. The only trouble was, my vision was blurry. Apparently I'd developed a minor case of snow blindness.

That five-hour stagger back to El Chaltén, crossing the glacier by postholing through knee-deep slush, was a real trudge. Once off the glacier, we stripped off all our wet clothing. Tired as we were, I was pretty frickin' happy. Later, other climbers would hail our Fitz Traverse as "cutting-edge alpinism." Rolo Garibotti himself, a man of few words and high standards, saluted us in print: "Respect, respect and more respect."

It didn't feel so cutting-edge to me. Tommy was always in good spirits, and we always got along. It felt like a really fun five-day camping trip with a good friend. I was proud of the fact that on the whole traverse—three and a half miles of travel, gaining and losing 13,000 feet of technical rock, snow, and ice—neither of us took a single fall.

•   •   •   •

The first climber to greet us in El Chaltén said, "Man, we were starting to worry about you guys." Something was wrong. Then we heard the news. Just two days earlier, Chad Kellogg, an extremely experienced forty-two-year-old American climber, had been killed on the descent from Fitz Roy, after climbing the Supercanaleta route. On rappel, he'd pulled loose a huge block that hit him on the head. He died instantly, with his partner, Jens Holsten, hanging right next to him. Holsten then had to complete the long descent alone.

Tommy knew Chad better than I did. In fact, I'd only barely met the guy. The tragedy hit Tommy hard. As he later wrote in Alpinist:

> We can tell ourselves that we minimize the dangers. Pick objec-
> tives that we're relatively certain we'll live through. Alex can cal-

culate every ropeless move with precision. I can choose to use a
rope. We can approach our climbing as a series of athletic goals or
as a quest for enlightenment. But the truth is, this kind of accident
could have happened to any of us. For the next few mornings in El
Chaltén, a hush appears to weigh on our little community of climbers. People wander the streets as if unsure of what to say. Each
night, we still congregate under the dim lights and rustic tables of
La Senyera and drink red wine. Gradually the laughter returns. But
when we talk about our climbs, it's with our heads down, our voices
low. The night seems to press against the windows, and the wind
shakes the door.

Kellogg's death also seemed to make Tommy reconsider extreme
climbing. He was thirty-five years old, and during the traverse he'd
thought often about Becca and one-year-old Fitz waiting for him to
return. As he concluded the essay for Alpinist,

On one hand I am still a kid, full of wonder at the world, chasing
dreams of distant summits. But I'm also a father—and this means I
am no longer allowed to die.

CHAPTER NINE
ABOVE AND BEYOND

Tommy Caldwell's father, Mike, *a serious climber in his own right, taught his son a lot of the tricks of the trade when he was very young. (Tommy was three years old when he started climbing.) A few years ago, he told me that his dad had said that he'd had about twenty-five close acquaintances die climbing. Now, in his midthirties, Tommy had his own grim roster of friends killed in the mountains or on the crags. On top of that, he'd undergone the nightmare ordeal of being kidnapped by rebels in Kyrgyzstan, marched through the mountains, and faced with the real likelihood that he was about to be executed.*

It was Tommy who'd pushed the rebel entrusted to guard him and his three fellow climbers off the cliff, allowing the four to escape. That act had weighed excruciatingly on his conscience. To help assuage his guilt, the other three agreed not to make public which one of them had performed the push. But Tommy couldn't live with that. Even before the four had reached the safety of a government camp, he'd insisted on taking responsibility for the critical act. When they found out later that the Kyrgyz guard had miraculously survived the fall, that news only minimally reduced Tommy's guilt, for they also learned that the man had been captured by government soldiers. If the poor guy is still alive—nobody seems to know—he's rotting away in prison for life.

By the age of twenty-eight, in contrast, I'd been relatively untouched by the tragedy of climbing buddies dying in accidents. The most significant death in my life up to that point had been that of my father, whose heart attack had taken him away when I was only nineteen. In some sense, I still hadn't completely absorbed or processed his disappearance.

About a month after I got home from Patagonia, however, there was terrible news out of Zion National Park. The way it came down was really hard on everybody who cared—and there were a lot of us.

Sean Leary had been my partner on some memorable climbs in Yosemite, including the linkup of three big walls in one day in 2010. He was also the guy who filmed me for Sender on the Great Roof on the Nose, then accompanied me by jugging his fixed rope the rest of the way up El Cap and joining me on the hiking approach to Half Dome, filming the whole way. And we'd had our friendly rivalry as we sought the speed record on the Nose, Sean teaming up with Dean Potter to break the record before Hans Florine and I broke it back.

Everybody called him "Stanley," a nickname he'd earned because he'd first climbed the Zodiac Wall on El Cap using a Stanley hammer—the kind you buy in a hardware store for carpentry. He didn't have a proper climbing hammer, but he was way psyched.

By 2014, besides being a world-class climber, Stanley had become a great BASE jumper. On March 13, he hiked alone to the top of a big cliff in the West Temple area of Zion. Because jumping is illegal in the national parks, he told almost no one about his plans, and he decided to launch at night, by the light of a full moon. He was using a wingsuit, so that he could steer his flight more or less as he chose on the way down.

Stanley was thirty-eight years old, happily married to Mieka, who was seven months pregnant with their first child. A week passed with no word from Stanley. Mieka simply thought he was somewhere out of cell-phone range. Only after he failed to show for a rigging job for a film company did anyone get alarmed. Then the only friend to whom he'd confided his plans spread the word, and Zion park rangers, along with some of Stanley's best friends, started searching the slopes below the cliff off of which they thought he might have jumped. All kinds of grim scenarios crossed their minds, the worst being that Stanley had died slowly and alone, hurt and disabled in the backcountry.

Ten days after Stanley had jumped, Dean Potter and others finally found his body. It was clear that he'd died instantly from some brutal blow. It was a jump that Stanley could have pulled off easily in the daytime, but, as Dean—a top BASE jumper himself—reconstructed the accident, he figured out what might have happened. Stanley had planned to fly through a V-notch formed by two buttresses a good ways down the cliff. As he approached the notch, he may have suddenly passed into the moon's shadow, as it was eclipsed by the cliff. Unable to see the rock, with only a second or two to correct his course, he probably clipped one of the walls and then failed to clear the notch. If he only bounced off one of the walls, that might have been survivable, but if the impact caused him to lose height and not clear the notch, that was inevitably fatal.

I wasn't very close to Stanley, but we were friends. His death seemed really tragic to me, especially with his first baby on the way. (Finn Stanley Leary was born two months after the accident.) At the same time—maybe I was rationalizing—I realized that a death like Stanley's had no bearing on the risks I ran as a climber. Everybody thinks free soloing is dangerous, but I think BASE jumping is way too dangerous.

I first tried skydiving—conventionally, with a parachute out of a plane—in 2010. I was, I'll have to admit, curious about BASE jumping. I thought that it might be a great way to make my linkups of big walls more efficient. I did eight or ten skydives and hated everything about them. I felt vaguely motion-sick on the bumpy plane rides up, crammed in with the other jumpers like sardines and breathing exhaust fumes. And I found falling out of a plane to be just plain scary. But mostly, the few jumps I did were enough for me to realize just how many it would take for me to feel comfortable and safe. A lot more skill and experience were required than I expected, and since I didn't really enjoy the learning process, I just decided BASE jumping wasn't for me.

I get asked all the time about risk. The usual questions are "Do you feel fear? Are you ever afraid? What's the closest you've ever come to death?" I get really tired of answering those questions over and over again. In all honesty, though, I can say that so far in climbing I've never come at all close to death—except for my absurd snowshoeing accident near Lake Tahoe in 2004. I've actually had closer calls driving than climbing, like once in a pea-soup fog in California's Central Valley, when I blew through a four-way stop I didn't see, locked up my brakes, and just slid right through. Or another time, also in the Central Valley, when a multi-car pileup forced me to lock up my brakes and plow around the wreck on the shoulder.

I have a take on risk and climbing that surprises a lot of people. I don't think it's the superdifficult climbs—even free solos—that will kill you. I think it's the sheer volume of moderate climbing that might cost you your life. John Bachar didn't die at age fifty-two because he was trying a free solo that was at his upper limit.

Instead, he fell off a route above his home in Mammoth Lakes that he'd climbed often, one that was well within his abilities. Whatever went wrong that day in 2009—whether it had to do with a back injury that had weakened his shoulder after his car accident, or whether he just slipped on a move he could normally have stuck, or whether a handhold broke—it may be that it was that sheer volume (three and a half decades of soloing) that finally caught up to him.

Paul Preuss, an Austrian born in 1886, was probably the first great free soloist. His idealism was so pure that he horrified his contemporaries, arguing, "With artificial climbing aids you have transformed the mountains into a mechanical plaything," and insisting that using a rope to get up a route was cheating. He actually thought soloing was safer than climbing roped—which, given the primitive gear and technique of the day, may well have been true. Back then, guys who fell while roped up often pulled their teammates to their deaths along with them.

Preuss died in 1913, at the age of twenty-seven, on a free-solo attempt on a new route on the Mandlkogel, a peak in the Austrian Alps. No one witnessed his thousand-foot fall, and his body wasn't discovered for a week, because new snows had covered it. But other climbers later found an open jackknife resting on the ridge crest near the point from which he must have fallen, which led them to propose an absurd but chilling scenario.

I can just picture it. Preuss stops for a lunch break. He takes out his knife, maybe to cut an apple or a hunk of cheese. The knife slips out of his hand, so he lunges forward to grab it, forgetting for an instant where he is. Goes off the edge, tries to grab something, and misses. Talk about the worst four seconds of his life!

The questions about fear also get tiresome, though I suppose they're natural. Mark Synnott recently told me an amusing story. It was after Mark, Jimmy Chin, and I had given a presentation in the Nat Geo Live! series in Explorers Hall at National Geographic Society headquarters in Washington, DC. There were three separate lines of folks wanting each of us to autograph posters. One of the guys in Mark's line was a neurobiologist. He leaned in close to Mark and said solemnly, "That kid's amygdala isn't firing."

The amygdala is the part of the brain that triggers the fight-or-flight response to danger. Apparently there's a rare genetic condition that destroys the amygdala. There's a famous case study of one such patient, called "The woman with no fear." Nothing the doctors probed her with—real spiders, real snakes, film clips of monsters and haunted houses—scared her at all. It wasn't surprising that by the age of forty-four, she'd gotten herself into, but managed to survive, all kinds of truly dangerous situations.

In my case, though, the neurobiologist had it all wrong. I'm every bit as capable of feeling fear as the next person. Danger scares me. But as I've told countless folks who ask, if I have a certain gift, it's the ability to keep myself together in places that allow no room for error. I somehow know, in such a fix—like the moves above Thank God Ledge on Half Dome where I stalled out in 2008—how to breathe deeply, calm myself down, and get on with it.

WHEN A CLIMBER—or, for that matter, any athlete or celebrity—gains such sudden stardom as Alex did after 2008, there's usually a backlash. It can come from rivals who think they need to put down the upstart threatening their own premier status, or from skeptics among the public who are all too willing to poke holes in the persona of the new phenom. In Alex's case, however, the backlash was faint and slow to materialize.

In part that might be attributed to Alex's genuineness. One observer after another was struck by how gracefully Alex handled his fame. Hand in hand with Alex's genuineness was his modesty, which at times could seem almost excessive. But "no big deal" was not a pose. Alex truly believes that there are better climbers than he in the cragging world—the Chris Sharmas and Adam Ondras who have climbed 5.15c, the Tommy Caldwells who have the patience and dedication to work a route for months or even years. And he believes that what he's done so far comes nowhere near the limits of what he's capable of.

Still, "no big deal" could strike even Alex's admirers as, if not an affectation, a nearly neurotic self-deprecation. At a North Face event in Boulder in August 2014, titled "The Relativity of Risk," Sender Films director Nick Rosen commented, "The only thing Alex does better than free soloing is downplaying. If that was a sport, he'd be in the Olympics." The audience cheered. Alex grinned sheepishly.

Along with his loyal fans, Alex motivated critics who were waiting for him to slip up and lay bare the vanity—or at least the craving for publicity—that they assumed must lie just under the surface of his professed indifference to adulation. In April 2013, Alex made just such a slipup—or seemed to, in the view of those quick-to-pounce critics. For the La Sportiva website, he wrote up a recent triumph of free soloing. It didn't help that the editors titled the piece "Alex Honnold—What a Day!" He began the piece: "On March 14th I free soloed three classic routes in Zion in a 12-hour day. It was the hardest free soloing effort I've put in."

The three solos were a repeat of Moonlight Buttress, followed by Monkey Finger (nine pitches up to 5.12b), rounded off with Shune's Buttress (eight pitches up to 5.11+). These were, Alex argued, "the three most classic free lines in Zion." Alex's original free solo of Moonlight Buttress in 2008 had thrust him into the media spotlight. Now, five years later, he had dispatched that climb as a mere one-third of a marathon day of soloing, the likes of which no one had dreamed of in Zion. "To sum it up in numbers," Alex concluded, "I did something like 30 pitches up to 12+ with 7 pitches of 5.12 and 8 pitches of 5.11. But the real crusher was that I hiked around 20 miles, much of it jogging downhill."

A fair assessment. The slipup, however, came in Alex's second paragraph:

> I could write several different essays about the day; it's given me a ton to think about. One would be how funny it is that climbing media didn't even touch the story and that no one seems to care about it. Soloing Astroman and the Rostrum in 2007 generated all kinds of news and video bits. This Zion link-up, which is infinitely harder and more cutting edge, doesn't get mentioned. That's what I get for soloing so much.

Alex's detractors seized upon these words, reading them as the petulant complaint of a superstar who, even as he pretended not to care about media plaudits, was hungry for more. Commenters on the La Sportiva site lavished praise on the deed itself. One blogged, "Awesome awesome awesome feat." But others demurred. "While it is an impressive feat of athletic skill and endurance," ventured one commenter, "it seems sad that the first impression I got was disappointment that the media hadn't been as impressed as you hoped, and that the climbing community wasn't standing in the aisles, cheering." Another blogger wondered, "Did anyone else find this obnoxious or condescending or whiny?"

Alex was stung by the reaction. Though he made no rebuttal to those jabs in print, privately he maintained that he had been misunderstood. "I wasn't complaining about lack of media attention," he says today. "What I was doing was really just pointing out how fickle the media can be. It just seems to be random what they single out for praise, what they ignore. If somebody's filming me on a solo, it becomes a media big deal. If I just go off and solo something by myself, nobody even asks me about it. That's fine with me. Media stuff honestly doesn't mean much to me."

Cedar Wright seconds this assertion. "There's so much amazing stuff Alex has done," he says, "that nobody knows about."

With fame and sponsorship came a ratcheting-up of demands on Alex's time to appear at company events, take part in panels, and speak at festivals. The "aggro" Alex of 2010, who could dismiss all those obligations as "media b.-s.," has since been tempered by the realization that the clamor of his fans is the price he has to pay for fame, and that fame is what allows him to lead a life as close to his heart's desire as he could concoct.

Even in 2010, for all his private griping about having to attend a North Face event or the Banff Mountain Film and Book Festival, Alex was unfailingly courteous when approached by fans. He never turned a cold shoulder on a kid wanting an autograph or an adult asking for a selfie shot with his hero in a café or campground.

If there was a single media event that elevated Alex's renown from the relatively insular climbing world to the arena of the general public, it was his appearance on *60 Minutes* in October 2011. Alex had come onto the radar of the producers of the CBS news show after they had seen Sender Films' *Alone on the Wall*. In a serendipitous pairing, they assigned the beautiful (and sometimes starstruck) Lara Logan to interview the climber, then twenty-six years old. The thirteen-minute segment *60 Minutes* delivered, though necessarily dumbed down for the nonclimbing audience, was a deft and appealing tribute to Alex.

Logan opens the piece with a tantalizing thesis: "From time to time we run across someone who can do something so remarkable that it defies belief . . . and in this case, seems to defy gravity." Rather than rely on footage from *Alone on the Wall*, the show organized a new free-solo climb by Alex: the north face of Sentinel Rock in Yosemite, via the 1,500-foot-long Chouinard-Herbert route, rated

5.11c. With the help of Sender's crew, the producers got fourteen different cameras in position beforehand to document Alex's feat.

Like *Alone on the Wall*, the *60 Minutes* piece toys with the conceit of Alex as a "dorky, awkward goofball" (Cedar Wright's appraisal in the Sender film) before he gets on the rock, where he's transformed into a genius. A photo of Alex as a young kid pops on the screen, to Logan's comment: "Back then, he was a shy, skinny kid with big ears." "The Ascent of Alex Honnold," as CBS titled its segment, skillfully intercuts climbing footage with tête-à-tête exchanges, some of them powerfully blunt. Logan asks, "Do you get an adrenaline rush?" Alex responds, "There is no adrenaline rush. If I get an adrenaline rush, it means that something has gone horribly wrong." The piece uses John Long as the Yosemite veteran and talking head. Logan asks Long what he considers Alex's greatest achievement. Long answers, "That he's still alive."

There's a priceless interlude in which Logan asks Alex about his unusually big hands. "Yeah, I have pretty big fingers," Alex admits, "so they're hard to get into a thin crack." "Show me," Logan coyly asks. Alex holds his hands out, palms up. Logan takes them in her own fingers, virtually fondling them. "Were they like this before you started climbing?" she asks girlishly. Alex seems oblivious to her flirtation.

From the perspective of *60 Minutes*, Alex's lifestyle seems unduly Spartan. Logan credits him for being "slow to cash in on his success," visits his van (expressing incredulity that he lives inside it), and seems astonished that he "survives on less than a thousand dollars a month." The day before the big show on Sentinel, Alex impulsively goes up to try to solo the Phoenix, the wildly overhanging 5.13a pitch above a drop to the Valley floor of at least 500 feet. Logan claims that he does so to "calm his nerves," but anyone who knows Alex recognizes that he's simply impatient and eager for yet another challenge.

As he recalls today, "I had been working on the Phoenix as a personal side project. I wanted to wrap it up before we got into full film mode—to do something truly hard for me before spending four or five days posing and filming and interviewing and generally fluffing about."

Only Peter Mortimer goes up to record the Phoenix. Beforehand, on camera, face-to-face with Logan, Alex claims he doesn't want "a bunch of people" hanging around that short but extreme free solo. "It'd be weird," he says. Logan: "It'd be weird? Why?" Alex, smiling: "I don't know. It would blow your mind. Just the positions [I'd get into] are outrageous." Logan clearly doesn't understand.

The climax of the segment unfolds on Sentinel Rock, with Lara Logan and John Long peering through scopes and binoculars from the meadow far below, as Long provides a blow-by-blow commentary. Long talks about a "point of no return" and the fifty-foot "crux of the whole route" near the top, while Logan cringes. Even Long gets freaked out when he sees that Alex has climbed into a runnel of flowing water on the route, and he watches as Alex tries to wipe dry the soles of his shoes on his opposite calves. As Alex heads into the key overhang, Long remarks that the footholds there are not good: "He'll have to paste his feet and hope they stick." Later, Alex himself will admit that getting his shoes wet was somewhat scary.

The close-up footage of the climbing, shot by pros, is superb, and there's nothing hokey about it. Sequences that Alex performs on Sentinel have every bit the power to make hard-core climbers' palms sweat that the comparable footage in *Alone on the Wall* and *Honnold 3.0* did.

Logan manages to wring at least one new insight out of the climber, as she wonders how much longer Alex can pursue free soloing at this level. "I don't think I'll continue to do this forever," Alex answers. "But I won't stop because of the risk. I'll stop just because I lose the love of it."

During the filming, Logan, producer Jeff Newton, and the rest of the CBS crew were both charmed and befuddled by Alex's lingo and his erratic behavior. So much so that they produced a *60 Minutes Overtime* pastiche of outtakes, titled "Dude: The Quirky World of Alex Honnold." The subhead read: "For *60 Minutes* producer Jeff Newton, shooting Alex Honnold's death-defying rock climbing was only part of the challenge. Jeff and the whole crew also had to learn Alex-speak, where everything is 'chill.'" The amusing clip focuses on Alex's possible overuse of four of his then-favorite words: *dude*, *chill* (both verb and adjective), *heinous*, and *mellow*. As Logan and Alex ride in his van, she interjects, startled, "Did you call me 'dude'?" Alex laughs and answers, "Yeah, you're gonna have to get used to that." According to Newton, in Alex's world, "everything is 'chill.'" So Logan asks, "What is chilling for you? How long can you chill for?"

The cameras follow Alex into his mother's house in Sacramento. Suddenly, he disappears. The crew finds him in a back room, opening boxes of free gear from The North Face. It's like Christmas, Logan muses. These "disappearances" may have nettled the crew during production, but now they're the source of mirth. "He was always doing pull-ups in the middle of the shoot," Newton marvels. Welcome to Alex's quirky world.

• • • •

From the little-known climber who once hoped that, as he put it, the attention of a sponsor might someday win him a free pair of rock shoes, Alex has by now developed into a thoroughgoing professional. One of his favorite quotes comes from the mouth of basketball legend Julius Erving: "Being a pro means doing what you love even on the days you don't love it."

Still, on any given Sunday, Alex would rather be climbing than signing autographs. In the spring of 2014, he agreed to serve on the film jury of the Trento (Italy) Film Festival. Only when he saw the schedule of presentations did he realize what he'd gotten himself into. "For Christ's sake," he confided in a few friends, "now I have to sit through thirty hours of Everest films. Totally heinous."

Wherever Alex appears nowadays, the event ends with long lines of admirers hoping to exchange a word or two with him and get him to sign a piece of memorabilia, usually a poster. "My default signature," Alex half-jokes, "is my name, plus 'Go big!'" (The signature is an efficient scrawl in which the only decipherable letters in his last name are "H" and "d," but Alex will lavish as many as three exclamation points on his touchstone injunction.) "I suppose," he adds, "I could write something like, 'Have a nice day climbing,' but that's just too many characters. 'Go big'—five characters. Exclamation marks are easy.

"At this one event, a really busty chick asked me to sign her boobs. 'Are you serious?' I asked. 'You bet,' she said, and pulled down her blouse, right there in public. No bra. So I signed my name on her left breast with a Sharpie. But after I stepped back to admire my handiwork, I felt like something was missing, so I added a 'Go big!!' to the right breast to even things out."

In November 2014, a bizarre turn of affairs rocked the American climbing world. Sender Films had completed *Valley Uprising*, a wild and woolly history of climbing in Yosemite that ran at nearly ninety minutes, mixing archival footage dating back to the 1950s with new clips shot for the movie. In a real sense, the film was Sender's magnum opus to date, and it was received with universal acclaim, winning the grand prize at all eight of the first film festivals in which it was entered. Needless to say, Alex's free soloing was prominently featured, as were Dean Potter's highball slacklining and deploying a BASE-jumping chute as a safety valve when he falls off overhanging walls.

The film debuted in Boulder on September 11, before a long-sold-out house. After that, it was screened in venues all across the United States and in Europe. But suddenly, in early November, Clif Bar—one of Alex's principal sponsors, as well as a sponsor of other leading climbers—announced that it was canceling support for five of its stars: Dean Potter, Steph Davis, Cedar Wright, Timmy O'Neill, and Alex. Apparently chief executives of the company had seen a showing of *Valley Uprising* in Berkeley, not far from company headquarters, on September 18, and they were not pleased. Ironically, Clif Bar was a major sponsor of the film itself. But it took the company almost two months to act.

In a carefully crafted statement, Clif Bar explained why it had fired some of its highest-profile adventurers: "We concluded that these forms of the sport are pushing boundaries and taking the element of risk to a place where we as a company are no longer willing to go."

All five climbers were taken completely by surprise. Says Alex, "I was up on a four-day climb on the Muir Wall in the Valley, and all of a sudden I was getting all these texts on my iPhone. I first heard about it from my mom. She wrote, 'Did you know you just got fired by Clif Bar?'"

The reaction in the climbing world was incredulous and derisive. Did the Clif Bar execs have no clue what it was that the climbers they sponsored were doing? Did it take watching *Valley Uprising* for them to wise up? After all, the company had sponsored Alex for the previous four years, Dean Potter for more than a decade.

The *New York Times* covered the controversy as the lead story on its sports page on Sunday, November 16. A photo of Alex free soloing in Yosemite—a still from the Sender Films shoot—took up the full half page above the fold. Reporter John Branch tried to cover the story evenhandedly, but the brunt of the criticism inevitably fell on Clif Bar. Dean Potter lashed out, "[W]hat they did was a filthy business move. . . . It seemed sleazy that Clif Bar would use some of my best climbs, and some of Alex's best climbs, as a marketing tool on one hand, but then fire us on the other." Cedar Wright complained, "It shows a lack of understanding for the sport, and a lack of respect for the athletes who have helped build their brand." As many observers pointed out, Clif Bar features a climber in silhouette on the cover of every one of its products.

Alex was asked to write an op-ed piece about the controversy for the *New York Times*. His piece appeared on November 20, four days after John Branch's news story. In it, Alex took a tempered and philosophical view of the fracas. He wrote,

> Of course, I was disappointed to be dropped by a sponsor, especially since I've always liked Clif Bar's product and really respect the company's environmental activism. And it did seem odd that after years of support, someone at Clif Bar seemed to have awakened suddenly and realized that climbing without a rope on vertical walls as high as 2,000 feet is dangerous.
>
> Still, I couldn't help but understand their point of view.

Alex cited another statement in the Clif Bar broadside: "This isn't about drawing a line for the sport or limiting athletes from pursuing their passions. We're drawing the line for ourselves." Then he explained: "In essence, that's the same way I feel when free soloing. I draw the lines for myself; sponsors don't have any bearing on my choices or my analysis of risk."

Alex ended the op-ed with a resounding affirmation of the risk-taking that lies at the heart of all adventure:

> Everyone needs to find his or her own limits for risk, and if Clif Bar wants to back away from the cutting edge, that's certainly a fair decision. But we will all continue climbing in the ways that we find most inspiring, with a rope, a parachute or nothing at all.

> Whether or not we're sponsored, the mountains are calling, and
> we must go.

The overwhelming majority of commenters on Clif Bar's action, even among nonclimbers, concluded that the company had simply blown it, in the process making fools of themselves. Many suggested a boycott. "I'm firing Clif Bar for stupidity," wrote a typical blogger. Yet the response to Alex's essay was more measured. He was widely praised for his restraint and magnanimity. Out of the debacle, he emerged unscathed.

• • • •

Toward the end of 2012, Alex and Peter Mortimer started tossing around the idea of filming an ascent of a building. As Mortimer later told *Outside* magazine, "We thought, wouldn't that be a rad next thing to do?" Alex agreed.

Soloing a skyscraper was not an original idea. For more than a decade, the French climber Alain Robert had made a career out of free soloing tall and iconic buildings, including the Eiffel Tower, the Sears (now Willis) Tower in Chicago, and the National Bank of Abu Dhabi. Since most countries outlaw skyscraper ascents, Robert ran the constant threat of getting arrested in midclimb—which happened more than once. As famous as his daring feats made him in France, however, Robert remains little known in the United States.

An American, "Spiderman" Dan Goodwin, had also made a name for himself in the 1980s, soloing such skyscrapers as the Sears Tower, but by 2012, his deeds were largely forgotten.

What Mortimer proposed, in order to make the project a novel one, was to film Alex's climb live. The extra *frisson* of watching an athlete in real time who might just possibly fall to his death was the kicker that got National Geographic Television on board. Next came the search for the right skyscraper. Self-evidently, the ascent would require not only the permission but the full cooperation of the authorities, so most of the buildings in the United States and Europe were out of the running. Also, according to Alex, "It was surprisingly hard to find something inspiring enough. A building that dominates the skyline and is actually worth climbing."

Alex and Pete first checked out the world's tallest skyscraper— Dubai's 2,717-foot Burj Khalifa. "Just the scout is a life-list experience," Alex told *Outside*. But he decided against the attempt, claiming, "The Burj was just too hardcore for me. It's the El Capitan of buildings."

Elaborating on his scout, he adds, "There's this little crack formed by the corners of the building that I couldn't get my fingers into at all. Instead, I had to pinch these opposing window frames that are maybe six feet apart and really slopey, so it made for very insecure climbing. Everything about it was just too much, the scale, the difficulty. The windows are plated glass, so it's like looking into a mirror as you climb, which is kind of scary since you see the skyline of the city laid out way below you. I heard that Dubai has something like sixty of the hundred tallest buildings in the world. Seeing them all down below you looking like toys is kind of unnerving, plus you see your own face, all sweaty and strained, looking right back at you from a few inches away.

"It's a hard building. Maybe someday. . . ."

From Dubai, Alex and Pete traveled to Taiwan to check out Taipei 101, at 1,667 feet then the world's second-tallest skyscraper. (Since 2012, two taller buildings have gone up, the Makkah Royal Clock Tower Hotel in Saudi Arabia and One World Trade Center in New York City; two others, both in China, are under construction.) Taipei 101 seemed to fit the bill. But the planned live TV broadcast—kept secret by Mortimer and National Geographic—was delayed for a year by logistics and bureaucratic red tape.

Meanwhile, in June 2013, Nik Wallenda tightrope-walked across the gorge of the Little Colorado River in Arizona. The event was broadcast live on the Discovery Channel, with a ten-second delay in case something went drastically wrong. The event was a huge media success, with thirteen million spectators tuning in, setting a thirteen-year record for the channel. Alex's skyscraper climb promised to be every bit as gripping and spectacular. Plans proceeded apace, and National Geographic Television went public with the news.

In December 2013, *Outside* ran a feature about the upcoming event. Grayson Shaffer's reporting was judicious, but the title and subtitle—"Alex Honnold Isn't Afraid of Skyscrapers" and "Climbing's biggest name makes his bid for international stardom by risking death on live TV"—smacked of tabloid journalism. For the lead photo, Alex dressed up as a Depression-era steelworker, complete with baker-boy cap, overalls, and suspenders atop his bare upper torso, lunch-bucket at his side, as he sat atop a girder seemingly hundreds of feet above the street. The photo was an homage to the famous black-and-white picture called "Lunch atop a Skyscraper" (often attributed to Lewis Hine but actually shot by Charles C. Ebbetts), which depicted eleven nonchalant workers sitting side by side eating lunch on a girder during the construction of Rockefeller Center in 1932. Depending upon one's taste, the Honnold parody came across as either clever or cheesy. Alex himself found the photo cheesy, but he adds, "I thought it was fun getting all dressed up and pretending to be an actor."

Shaffer asked Alex how much he was being offered by National Geographic to perform the stunt. He reported, "Honnold won't discuss specific figures, but he acknowledges that he'll be paid 'vastly more than anything I've encountered in the climbing world' for the project."

Response to the *Outside* article was mixed. Along with the usual cheers from the sidelines ("Big time goal, Alex. Bravo"), there were murmurs of disappointment. For perhaps the first time in his career, the pithy phrase *selling out* was associated with Alex Honnold. Wrote one *Outside* commenter, "What sucks is the greatest climber who ever lived now has to resort to climbing a building for cash? . . . It might be fun to watch on the news, but to climbers I feel like it's treason." And another: "It's fine if you want to climb a building for money, but don't try to convince me that you are doing [it] because you are inspired."

The same *New York Times* editor who would later assign to Alex the op-ed piece about the Clif Bar imbroglio asked this writer [David Roberts] in early 2014 to structure an op-ed piece around the very question of whether the skyscraper project was evidence that Honnold was selling out. I declined. When I e-mailed Alex to tell him about this development, he responded, "I wouldn't actually mind if you wrote something like that. I think it's fair enough to take criticism for those kinds of projects. I think you would be wrong, but it never hurts to have a spirited argument." In the same way that he would later rise above the Clif Bar controversy, Alex welcomed a debate about whether Taipei 101 was corrupting his values as well as those of the climbing community.

In the end, the whole controversy became moot. National Geographic started to freak out about the cost of the production, and when the institution undertook a periodic cleansing of its house in the spring of 2014, new personnel less enthusiastic about the skyscraper climb pulled the plug on the society's support. Even before that, though, Alex had balked at some of the conditions. "They wanted me to wear a parachute, which is ridiculous," he says. "I tried to tell them that a chute wouldn't do a bit of good if I fell off, because I'd hit one of the projecting balconies long before I could deploy it, but they just didn't get it. They were all hung up on risk. They didn't want me dying on live TV."

But Peter Mortimer isn't giving up. He envisions filming Alex's solo of Taipei 101 sometime in 2015 or 2016—not for live TV but for a film like *Alone on the Wall*. And Alex is still enthusiastic about the challenge. "I don't think the climb would be super-hard," he says. "Climbing on a building is a lot like training in a climbing gym—repetitive moves that emphasize pure fitness more than anything else. But it's still cool to get on top of such a big building. And in some ways the view is even better than in the mountains, just because the urban environment has so much going on."

• • • •

In the first two months of 2014, Alex had accomplished two of the greatest challenges of his climbing life—the free solo of El Sendero Luminoso and the Fitz Traverse. He didn't have anything else quite that big on his agenda for the rest of the year, but he wanted to climb as much as he could. The hunger was still there.

In March, Alex and Cedar Wright met up near Grand Junction, Colorado, to attempt what they called *Sufferfest 2*. *Sufferfest 1* had been shot in June 2013 in California, as Alex and Cedar climbed all fifteen of the state's 14,000-foot peaks—from Mount Shasta in the north to Mount Langley in the south—biking between peaks rather than using any motorized transport. Adding to the challenge was the fact that both men were basically novice cyclists. In the hands of a more solemn filmmaker, the ordeal could have been staged as a heroic marathon, but Cedar's vision was to portray the trip as an exercise in absurdity, with "suffering" as a comic end in its own right.

The pair pulled off the challenge, biking some 700 miles, hiking about 100, and climbing a total of 100,000 vertical feet in twenty-two days. All the climbing on the 14-ers—most of it by nonstandard routes—was free soloing, up to grades as stiff as 5.10c. Alex and Cedar pretty much wrecked their bodies in the process. On White Mountain, the guys had to bike ninety miles round trip and gain and lose 11,000 vertical feet. As Cedar told *Climbing* magazine, "It was *brutal*. Even Honnold had a moment of wanting to give up."

The film played the two warriors as innocents abroad, trying to figure out how to make their bikes work but cavorting gleefully on sometimes chossy arêtes and ridges in the Sierra Nevada. The tone was manic and playful. Yet there was no ignoring the severity of the punishing ordeal. As Cedar reflected for *Climbing,*

> I consider this to be one of the greatest achievements of my climbing life, and it was awesome to share it with Honnold, who is a great friend and motivating force in my life. Mostly we toiled and suffered, but occasionally I would have a moment of genuine bliss, taking in the beauty of the incredible Sierra Nevada. It was a full-on sufferfest, but I think in a couple of weeks I'll look back on this as fun.

For *Sufferfest 2,* Cedar would craft a film around another zany, self-imposed endurance challenge: The idea was to try to climb forty-five desert towers in Colorado, Utah, New Mexico, and Arizona in three weeks, bicycling between objectives as he and Alex covered more than 800 miles on paved highways, marginal back roads, and single-track trails.

To make the film, Cedar hired a small crew of riggers and cameramen, including Hayden Kennedy, one of the best alpinists and rock climbers of Alex's generation. But none of the filming would be rehearsed or reenacted—the crew had the task of capturing the action as it unfolded.

Nine months after their romp in the Sierra Nevada, Cedar and Alex concocted a similar orgy of self-mutilation via nonstop biking and climbing among the desert towers of the Southwest. But this time, the journey—and the film—would culminate with a project born of Alex's philanthropic concerns, as embodied by the Honnold Foundation. At the end of their sufferfest, Cedar and Alex would join with a company called Eagle Energy to install solar-energy panels in a number of hogans and houses on the Navajo Reservation in Arizona, bringing power and light to traditional Native Americans, some of whom had lived their whole lives without electricity or running water.

The tone of the film, as of the adventure, is stamped on its title screen: "Thirty Four Pieces of Choss & Five Horrendous Life Experiences." The online teaser summarizing the video goes on in the same vein: "Any terrible idea is worth repeating . . . especially if like Alex Honnold and Cedar Wright you have a terrible memory and seem to remember your last 'sufferfest' as not too bad." And it salutes the "goofy duo" as they embrace "60mph winds, loose rock and even looser ideas of what is safe." Alex appears on screen, predicting, "I think it's going to be fun. . . . No, it's definitely going to be bad." Followed by Cedar's take: "Oh my God, we learned nothing from the last trip?"

Cedar and Alex start *Sufferfest 2* with an ascent of what they hail as the first desert tower ever climbed—Independence Monument, a 450-foot sandstone spire near Grand Junction, Colorado. Therein lies a bizarre story. Way back in 1911, a madman named John Otto carved and pounded holds in the soft rock as he tamed the tower by creating an artificial staircase up it. On July 4, he flew the Stars and Stripes from the summit. The tradition persists more than a century later, as climbers tackle the spire on Independence Day and fly their own American flags from the top. Otto went on to become the first caretaker of Colorado National Monument, earning the princely salary of one dollar per month well into the 1920s.

Alex and Cedar scamper up "Otto's Route" on Independence Monument, rating it solid 5.9, as they marvel over the holes and steps carved in the rock so long ago. As Alex later reported, "I thought it was an amazing route—historic and fun."

Riding their hybrids (crosses between road and mountain bikes) into Utah, they get lost on the way to the Fisher Towers. Much of the comedy of the film spins off the still somewhat rudimentary skills of the "goofy duo" as cyclists.

The Fisher Towers are the epitome of choss. Alex and Cedar set their sights on the Titan, the tallest of the several pinnacles—in fact, it's the tallest freestanding tower in the United States. The route they choose, called Finger of Fate, was put up more than half a century ago by the legendary Layton Kor, who rated it 5.8 A2. It's one of the great classic lines in the Southwest, but it's seldom climbed free, because it goes only at 5.12d.

On film, gazing up at the Titan, Alex intones, "Choss is like the inclusive term for all things bad about rock climbing." Cedar chimes in: "It's like crazy melted wax. Petrified candles." Alex: "It's really beautiful to look at, but really frightening to climb." On the route, as they come across antiquated bolts the likes of which they've never seen before, they chalk it up to a "history lesson."

And then the wind—the predictable bane of hiking and climbing in the Southwest in the spring—starts lashing the spire. The partners have to scream to communicate. The rope trailing behind them sails out horizontally across the face. On the summit, Alex stares into the camera and pronounces, "It's kind of apocalyptic. The world could be ending around us. And we are"—he searches for the word—"shell-shocked."

The canny skill of Cedar's filmmaking comes to the fore in scenes such as these. What could easily be played as epic melodrama comes across—suffering and all—as antic fun. Everything is part of the game. In their scariest and tiredest moments, the guys still keep tongues firmly in cheeks.

Looking back on the journey half a year later, however, Alex remembers a more serious mood that haunted the road trip as he and Cedar pedaled onward through the night. Three days into *Sufferfest 2*, they got the news about Sean "Stanley" Leary's death while BASE jumping in Zion. Stanley had been Alex's frequent partner and good friend, but he had been even closer to Cedar—had in fact been the mentor who taught Cedar how to climb.

As Alex explains, "We found out about his death after we rapped off the Finger of Fate. The film crew had hung around to tell us the news, so as soon as we got down off the Titan and were about to pull our rappel ropes, Hayden Kennedy came up and told us what had happened in Zion. Cedar was super-choked. He threw some things around and cursed a lot. I was a lot more subdued, but I was pretty choked myself.

"We all hiked out together and talked a lot about life and loss. We decided that we would carry on to the next destination and keep on going with the Sufferfest, rather than bail to Zion to participate in the grieving and the body recovery. So we ate some dinner in camp, talking more about all these things, then Cedar and I got on our bikes and rode the fifteen miles west to Castleton Tower. It was cold and dark and it was just the two of us riding under the stars. Dark and stark in the desert. We'd spent all day getting worked with the cold wind and scary climbing, so we were feeling fragile anyway. So it felt like a really powerful thing to be questing through the night together, ruminating on what Stanley should have done differently and what it all meant.

"The desert is sort of a reflective place anyway—that's why Jesus went there to do his heavy thinking. The loneliness, the darkness, the bleakness. It's a poignant place to think about mortality and the meaning of life. Not that we came up with anything profound, other than the fact that Stanley would have kept climbing, and so would we. And that we wished he hadn't been a BASE jumper."

• • • •

Cedar and Alex climb Castleton Tower and then push onward to Monument Basin, where they get sandbagged on a weird leaning tower called the Shark's Fin. A friend named Rob Pizem had recommended the route. As Cedar complains in the film, "What he said was, 'You should do it, it's a super-fun, easy route.' What he should have said was, 'It's a lot of hard, overhanging climbing, and you could die.'" Alex: "Next time I see him, I'm going to punch him in the nose." Alex and Cedar were able to climb most of the spires in around one hour each. The Shark's Fin took about six.

For days on end, the wind never lets up. Some of the best footage captures the guys biking through dust storms, or collapsed on the ground, trying to rub the sand out of their eyes. "Who needs Patagonia," asks Cedar rhetorically, "when you can come to the desert in the spring?" By now the adventure has become an homage to extreme fatigue, as Alex and Cedar beg each other for a rest day. Forty-five towers in three weeks, of course, is an arbitrary goal, but so was the Triple Crown in under twenty-four hours. So the pair stick with the program.

Alex falls off his bike in the night and incurs a really nasty scrape on his right buttock. Fodder for more comic footage. The guys bike west to climb the twin Sixshooter peaks near Indian Creek and find superb crack climbing on Bridger Jack Mesa. Good rock instead of choss at last, but one of the scariest pitches of all comes in a body-size squeeze chimney that Alex leads near the summit of North Sixshooter. "This is awesome," Alex announces, and Cedar rubber-stamps the pitch as "legitimately super-hardcore."

Into New Mexico to climb the isolated volcanic dike of Shiprock, sacred to the Navajo. As Cedar steps off the dirt road to take a leak, he discovers a tiny black puppy in the ditch. It's a classic "Rez dog," abandoned by its owner. The roly-poly dog becomes the team mascot, following the men throughout the rest of the trip and earning its nickname of Sufferpup. Cedar holds the stupefied dog in his hands, shaking it as he brays, "I'm a bear! I'm a bear!" The men fashion a kennel out of a Tecate twelve-pack box, to be transported in the camera crew's car.

As they had the previous year, Alex and Cedar meet their self-imposed challenge of forty-five towers in twenty-one days. But the levity of the film tends to disguise just how serious the climbing gets at times. In *Sufferfest 2*, the guys do almost no free soloing. You don't free solo on choss, Alex's manic pranks in Chad notwithstanding. One of the last towers the two climb is called the Whale, the quintessence of choss. Alex knocks loose huge chunks of sandstone as he leads, and the camera follows the plunging rocks as they strike ledges and burst apart, taking more pieces of the tower with them. "One of the most disgusting things I've done," comments Alex about the climb.

Unlike *Sufferfest 1*, the desert film now turns to its more serious rationale, which Alex previews by pointing out, "Our trip is probably easier than most people's lives."

They're done with climbing. Now the purpose of the voyage transforms into public service, as Alex and Cedar go to work on their solar-energy project on the Navajo Reservation near Monument Valley. They team up with Eagle Energy, a domestic offshoot of a nonprofit called Elephant Energy, whose main business is in Namibia. (Since there are no elephants in Arizona, the company adopted the eagle for its Southwestern program.) Further support comes from Goal Zero, The North Face, Clif Bar, and Alex's own Honnold Foundation.

In 2013, Eagle Energy had distributed small-scale solar systems through local entrepreneurs near Tuba City, also on the reservation. There's an additional educational component, as Eagle teaches kids about solar energy. What Alex and Cedar do in March 2014 is to hook up the houses and hogans of elderly and impoverished Navajos free of charge, as a way of demonstrating to the community that solar "works." In the film, the two climbers clamber across rooftops fitting their panels, then turn on lights inside the dwellings, as the faces of the residents beam with wonderment and surprise.

The work on the reservation fits Alex's broader environmentalist outlook. As he puts it, "You can take tiny little steps toward a bigger objective. With small efforts like our Navajo project, you can slowly work toward the bigger goals of transitioning to a carbon neutral world and lifting people out of poverty. Things that seem prohibitively hard when you look at the scale of the total problem, but more reasonable once you start to chip away at it."

Seven months after their desert ramble, Cedar's twenty-six-minute film, *Sufferfest 2*, dedicated to Sean "Stanley" Leary ("our guru in suffering"), wins the People's Choice Award at the prestigious Banff Mountain Film and Book Festival. Cedar is delighted, even overwhelmed by the honor. He also feels that all the hard work he'd put in to make the film is validated by the award.

Sufferfest 2, indeed, is a gem. Audiences laugh and cheer as they watch it, and when it's over, they're left wanting more. Above all, the film is a vivid testimony to friendship. Close friendship to begin with, made stronger and more lasting by adversity, uncertainty, risk, and—yes, the absurd point of it all—suffering in all its glory.

Four months after our biking and climbing marathon in the Southwest, Dave Allfrey and I teamed up in Yosemite for what we called the "7 in 7" challenge. The idea was Dave's, or at least it was suggested to him by a couple of friends. The challenge was to try to climb seven different routes on El Cap in seven days. It would be a gigantic test not only of our ability to simul-climb and jug efficiently but also of our stamina. Once Dave proposed it, I was all in.

Dave is the same age as I am, but he has a lot more experience than I do with alpine and big-range mountaineering. He's also a much better aid climber than I am, and that would be vital on our

7 in 7 campaign. He loves to remind me that he holds more El Cap speed records than I do, owing to the fact that he's climbed so many of the hard aid lines. In fact, I'm a pretty terrible aid climber. I've only hammered three pitons in my life—in the spring of 2014 on those rotten desert towers—and I have no idea how to place copperheads.

Dave and I had climbed together a fair amount in Yosemite before 2014. On El Cap, we'd teamed up to set speed records on three different routes—Excalibur, Lunar Eclipse, and the West Buttress.

On July 2, 2014, we headed up our first route, New Jersey Turnpike—the hardest of the seven, rated 5.10 A4. Unfortunately, the Valley was in the midst of a heat wave, and the temps got up to 95 degrees Fahrenheit each day. That just made everything harder.

On the Turnpike, we played to our strengths: I led all the free and mixed pitches, Dave led all the aid. Instead of the normal start, we chose the El Nino variation, which has some stiff 5.13b slab climbing on it. We chose this alternate start because we thought I could French free 13b faster than Dave could climb the A4 on the standard start. And it seemed like way more fun. Turns out it was pretty run-out, and I took a huge thirty-foot whipper on the first hard pitch, but after that I managed to squeak through.

The crux came high on the route, where Dave took the lead on back-to-back A4 pitches on nasty black diorite. A4 (on the scale that runs from A0 to A5) is serious. It means your gear is pretty crappy, and if you rip one piece there's a chance you'll rip a whole series. At worst, you'd take a long fall and have to count on your partner's belay and anchor to stop you.

Here Dave came into his element, as he gingerly moved through loose rocks, sharp flakes, bad rivets (shallow boltlike doodads driven only far enough into the rock to hold your body weight), and old copperheads left in place by previous parties. Each pitch took Dave forty-five minutes to lead. After that, we got back onto the more typical orange-and-white granite of El Cap. I led the rest of the way, including an infamous poorly protected 5.9 pitch led by Ron Kauk on the first ascent in 1977. We topped out in twelve hours and twenty-eight minutes—more than an hour and a half faster than the previous speed record.

Trying to beat the worst of the heat, we started each climb at 4:00 a.m. Even though we tried to go to bed each evening by 7:30 p.m., it never felt like we got enough sleep. Already on the morning of July 3, we were tired from the previous day's effort.

Our second route was Tangerine Trip, a slightly shorter line on the southeast face of El Cap. It's not super-hard—rated at 5.8 A2. I felt like I was getting into the swing of things, leading free and mixed pitches pretty efficiently. We got up the Trip in nine hours and twenty-eight minutes, also a new speed record. And on the third day we did Eagle's Way in seven hours and fifty-six minutes—our third speed record in a row.

Part of what made 7 in 7 so grueling was that after each ascent, we had to hike down the East Ledges, nearly 3,000 feet to the Valley floor, then circle around to our car. Dave had a bad night after Eagle's Way. As he later wrote for Alpinist, "I awoke in the night with numb fingers and a pain in my left hand and elbow. The ache kept me awake for several hours, stealing much-needed sleep. Luckily the pain receded with icing."

Fortunately, in the morning Dave was still game to continue our quest. On July 5, our fourth day, we climbed the Nose. Of course we had no intention of going for the speed record there— after all, it had taken a lightning blitz by Hans Florine and me to set the record of 2:23:46 in 2012. Climbing well, Dave and I got up the Nose in five and a quarter hours. Since that was our fastest route so far, it gave us the luxury of a much-needed afternoon of rest. Down on the Valley floor, we spent several hours hydrating, eating, and soaking our hands and legs in the Merced River. Then we headed to our friend Ken Yager's house in El Portal, just outside the national park, where we took showers, ate dinner, and crashed for the short night.

Lurking Fear and Zodiac were our next two objectives. They seemed pleasant and even easy compared to what we'd already done, and we dispatched them both in exactly five hours and five minutes. As Dave later told Climbing magazine, "It was just grinding out trade routes as fast as we could, getting down to the river to ice our hands and legs, eating and sleeping. Then getting up way too early to do it all again."

On July 8, we faced the last of our seven routes, the Triple Direct. It's rated 5.9 A1, not too severe, but it's a long route—3,200 feet of climbing over thirty-five pitches if you tackled it in conventional style. As tired as we were, we wanted to try to set another speed record, and when we got to the top in five hours and fifteen minutes, we pulled it off. I'm sure the route could be climbed faster, but Dave said he was pretty pleased that after 173 guidebook pitches spread over the seven days, we still had the stamina and drive to improve on the fastest time.

Even though 7 in 7 wasn't the ultimate feat of marathon Yosemite climbing, it was pretty gratifying. We got our partnership honed to close to perfection. As Dave later wrote in Alpinist,

> In the end I believe we found what we were looking for—a physical and mental endurance challenge and a grand adventure on El Capitan. We hoped to enchain in-a-day ascents and find a new level of difficulty. We wanted to test our big-wall skill and efficiency to see if we could make this possible. We were both proud to see the whole week through, and glad when it was over.

Covering our 7 in 7 for Rock and Ice, Chris Parker asked me if I thought we could ever improve on that string of big-wall climbs. I answered, "I'm not sure how we would exactly. Of course I'll want to do harder things in the future, but I definitely wouldn't want to climb 10 in 7 or something. That would just be boring."

For the moment, I'd had enough. "It's been fun," I told Parker, "but now that we're done with the El Cap mission I'm going to become a sport climber again."

A couple of days later, Cedar Wright phoned me for an interview for the North Face website. He asked some straight questions, such as what it was like to climb with Dave. I answered, "Awesome. Always motivated and always in high spirits. And more importantly, he's probably one of the best aid climbers in the world. I don't think a mission like this would have been possible with anybody else."

Cedar knows all about speed climbing, but, playing the dutiful reporter, he asked me why I was drawn to it. "I think the thing that I like most," I answered, "is how efficiently it all goes. Speed climbing forces you to trim all the waste out of your systems and to streamline all the processes. As a result, the climbing feels very smooth—and that's a great feeling."

Then Cedar stuck the needle in. "Why didn't you guys do more difficult routes?" he deadpanned. I knew he was just trying to get my goat, but I gave him a straight answer: "We thought about ending with a hard aid line, possibly a route that had never been done in a day. But ultimately, it just seemed like more fun to finish the mission with Triple Direct and still be down in time to do a picnic in the meadow."

Cedar wasn't done with the needle. Now he asked me, "Have you found the contraband I stashed in your van yet from when I borrowed your wheels while you were in Europe?"

This for the normally straightforward and serious North Face website! So I needled him back, "Other than the hideously disgusting throw pillows that you left on the bed, I don't think there is any contraband in the van."

• • • •

As I write these pages, I'm four months past my twenty-ninth birthday. Some folks have asked me whether I might have already reached my prime. After all, in professional sports, most athletes peak between about twenty-five and twenty-eight. That Roger Federer can still win a tennis tournament at age thirty-three is regarded as miraculous. A lot of baseball owners think that giving a pitcher or a shortstop who's over thirty a long-term contract is a mistake. It's a cruel reality, but the stats seem to back up those pessimistic assessments.

All it takes is the sudden arrival on the scene of a young hotshot to make you feel old. When I was climbing at Smith Rock in Oregon in the fall of 2010, a gang of top French climbers showed up. The prodigy in their ranks was a fifteen-year-old kid named Enzo Oddo. He'd already made a big splash in France, where he'd led seven 5.14d routes in the previous year. Too young to drive a car, he was chaperoned and belayed by his mother. He just seemed like a happy-go-lucky youngster having fun in the playground. But at Smith, he was climbing surely and beautifully.

I was twenty-five at the time. "Enzo's the shit," I told my friends admiringly. But watching him climb, I suddenly felt old. I remembered when I was that young kid on his way up.

I know there are plenty of folks—both friends and fans—who think I'm simply rolling the dice with my free soloing. As well as he knows me, and as fruitfully as we've worked together, Pete Mortimer talks about his doubts as to whether he should continue to film my solos. Last year he told a writer, "There's a loud chorus out there of people who are not comfortable with what Alex is doing. Even some of his partners think there's a good chance he's going to kill himself."

When Stacey and I were first dating and I was teaching her to climb, she always said she wasn't worried about me killing myself. "I feel Alex is totally in control," she told a writer in 2010. But then one day she was watching me as I tried to onsight solo a 5.12a stem corner. I went up and down as I worked it out. Naturally, it was scary to watch. And scary to do, for that matter. After that, Stacey decided she didn't want to watch that kind of stuff any more.

The odd thing is, it's harder to watch free soloing than to do it.

I gave a talk at the Harvard Travellers Club in Boston in 2011. Mostly it amounted to screening Alone on the Wall. I was sitting next to a woman in the audience who asked me a question that nobody else had yet posed. "I know that you don't get anxious when you're free soloing," she said. "But what's it like to watch yourself solo on film?"

"My palms sweat," I had to admit.

There have also been people, including several writers, who have wondered out loud whether my sponsors and the media are pushing me to keep risking my life. But I think they're wrong. Nobody says to me, "Hey, Alex, can you go out and solo harder and harder routes?" Nobody wants me to solo, except me.

I probably can't judge objectively whether, at twenty-nine, I've reached or even passed my prime. You tell a baseball or football player that he's over the hill at thirty-two, and he'll get blue in the face trying to prove he isn't. But right now, I really do feel that I'm just coming into my best years. I think my finest climbs are still ahead of me. I haven't yet pushed myself to the limit, but, even more important, I've still got a burning desire to climb that's as intense as it ever was. There are so many great challenges out there, on walls and peaks all over the world. I feel just the way I did when I dropped out of Berkeley at nineteen, that there's nothing else in life that's half as interesting as climbing.

So what are those challenges that might inspire me in the near future? For years now, everybody's been talking about the first free solo of El Cap. I've thought about it for years myself. In my journals, as early as 2009, there are entries like "Check out Freerider," or "Check out Golden Gate." The problem with free soloing El Cap is that it's so much bigger even than Half Dome, and there are no all-free routes easier than 5.12d. I'm not surprised that nobody has yet even attempted a free solo of El Cap. I think it's possible, but you'd have to be really ready. You'd have to really want it. The hardest thing would be just getting off the ground. But it would be amazing.

For a while, the media flirted with the idea that Dean Potter and I were rivals to pull off the first free solo on El Cap. I just shrugged off that talk, but it sort of pissed Dean off. "Let's talk about it after it's happened," he told Outside in 2010. "The magazines want a race. But this would go beyond athletic achievement. For me, this would be at the highest level of my spirituality."

By now, because I'm so well recognized in the Valley, it wouldn't be possible to work a route—rehearsing all the moves with a rope and a partner in preparation for a free solo—without attracting a lot of attention. If the word got out—"Alex is getting Freerider dialed so he can try to solo it"—it would be a gigantic distraction. Back in 2008, when I free soloed Moonlight Buttress and Half Dome, nobody knew who I was. I had the good luck to rehearse those climbs without anybody making a fuss, and the even better luck to climb them when nobody else was on the routes.

For that matter, even El Cap wouldn't be the ultimate free solo. On Nameless Tower, a huge granite spire in the Trango Towers group of the Karakoram Range in Pakistan, there's an amazing route called Eternal Flame. It's as big as El Cap, and it starts at 17,000 feet above sea level. The route was put up in 1989 by a very strong German foursome, including Wolfgang Gullich and Kurt Albert. After lots of other climbers tried and failed, the Huber brothers, Alex and Thomas, succeeded in climbing it all free in 2009. They rated it 5.13a. Claiming they were lucky to have good weather and find almost no ice in the cracks, the Hubers called Eternal Flame "the best and most beautiful free climb on the globe." If there's a challenge for the proverbial "next generation," it would be free soloing Eternal Flame.

I suppose it's inevitable that most of the media attention I get is for free soloing. But I'm just as proud of my speed climbs and link-ups. Even though they aren't as glamorous, and don't really capture the public imagination the same way, they represent the same spirit as soloing. Covering a ton of ground as simply as possible. They are all just by-products of a desire to climb a lot.

A few years ago, when I was flipping past all the pictures in Alpinist with snow in them, I swore I'd never go mountaineering. But here I am, having already gone on two big-range expeditions— to the Ruth Gorge in Alaska in 2013 and the Fitz Roy massif in Patagonia in 2014. Tommy Caldwell and I had such a great time on the Fitz Traverse that we started planning another big Patagonian enchainment for February 2015. We wanted to attempt the Torre Traverse—a linkup of four amazing towers culminating in Cerro Torre (once called "the hardest mountain in the world"). It wouldn't be a first, because Rolo Garibotti and Colin Haley nailed it in 2008. But there's a lot more ice on the Torre Traverse than we ran into on the Fitz Traverse—especially the hideous rime mushroom cap on Cerro Torre—and Tommy and I aren't veteran ice climbers.

It took Rolo and Colin four days to make the traverse, as they gained and lost almost 7,000 feet of elevation on steep rock and

near-vertical rime ice. The scariest part of their marathon climb
came as they headed up the El Arca route on Cerro Torre. As Rolo
later wrote in the American Alpine Journal,

> Then, suddenly, it was too warm. Ice fell around us, crashing
> against the rock with the sound of waves. For the next two hours
> we climbed as fast as possible, ducking our heads, until we found
> a rock prow under which we could find shelter. It was only 5 p.m.,
> but we decided to stop and bivy.

The next morning, in colder, safer conditions, they climbed the El
Arca route and completed the traverse.

Tommy and I thought it would be cool to see whether we could
repeat the Torre Traverse, no matter how long it might take. If we
managed to do it at all, it would be a crowning achievement in
both of our climbing careers, largely because it would be so different from what we normally attempt.

But then, on January 14, 2015, Tommy and Kevin Jorgeson
finally completed the first free ascent of the Dawn Wall on El
Cap. Before topping out, they spent nineteen straight days on the
wall, sleeping on a portaledge, as they painfully worked their way
through each of the route's thirty-one pitches, including the 5.14
cruxes on pitches 14, 15, and 16. I was not only rooting constantly
for those guys—I jugged up the fixed ropes to chat with them and
supply them with snacks.

The climb got huge attention worldwide, including front-page
coverage several days running in the New York Times, as well as a
shout-out from President Obama. Nobody argued with the indis-
putable fact that Tommy and Kevin had put up the hardest free
big-wall rock climb in the world. My admiration for Tommy simply
swelled to a new dimension. The guy's an amazing hardman,
climbing better than he ever has at age thirty-six.

In the frenzy of media attention that the Dawn Wall stirred up, however, with Tommy besieged by agents wanting him to write a memoir and producers hoping to film his life story, he had to back out of Patagonia. I decided to head down there anyway, still hoping to find a partner to attempt the Torre Traverse.

During a stormy three weeks last February, I paired up with Colin Haley, who was game to try to repeat his own Torre Traverse with me. The weather didn't cooperate, though we made several good ascents, including Torre Egger in fast alpine style. Colin had not only first completed the Torre Traverse with Rolo Garibotti in 2008, but he had since repeated it in the opposite direction (south to north), so it was only for my sake that he was willing to give it a third go. During our weeks together, he and I had a whole list of objectives. I suggested trying to do the Torre Traverse in one 24-hour blitz. (Colin's two previous jaunts had taken about four days each.) We agreed that that was the most exciting project to focus on.

Despite mists, wind, running water on the rocks, and lousy ice conditions, we got over Standhardt, Punta Herron, and Torre Egger in really good time. At 7:30 p.m. we started up Cerro Torre in the waning light. Halfway up, it got truly dark, so we climbed on with headlamps. We got only two pitches short of the summit before the storm really socked in.

For two hours, we hung out in a wretched nook, half-hanging from our harnesses. We were waiting for the first light of dawn, so that we could see how stormy it really was. In the dark all we could tell was that there was a crazy strong wind and we couldn't see any stars. It felt like it was about to snow. According to the forecast, the storm wasn't due for another 24 hours, but it had actually arrived way ahead of time.

At last we decided to bail. Colin thought that rapping the complicated and exposed north face in these conditions would be too dangerous, so we made an emergency descent of the west face. Then we had a soul-destroying march through the Paso Marconi. The whole adventure lasted 53 hours, with no stove or bivy gear the whole way, and the last twenty hours without food, before we got back to El Chaltén.

As Colin wrote the next day, "It's unfortunate that we didn't quite get to finish the goal, but I'm very pleased with our performance, knowing that if the weather had held out we would've easily finished within a cool 24 hours of starting. Despite failing, it is probably the best day of climbing I've ever done in these mountains, and it certainly turned into the most epic experience I've had here."

• • • •

If there's a great range I haven't visited that intrigues me, it's the Karakoram. I could see trying big walls in the Trango group. I'd love to bring Yosemite-style in-a-day tactics to some of the biggest faces in the world. The highest I've been so far is only 19,341 feet, on the summit of Mount Kilimanjaro in Tanzania, at the end of what amounted to a long stroll. I'd kind of like to see if I could still perform well above 20,000 feet.

The media are fond of talking about the "ultimate limits" of adventure. I sort of follow other "sports," like big-wave surfing, or huge waterfall drops in kayaks, or crazy mountain biking. Guys (and gals) are doing unbelievable things in those realms. It's hard to imagine improving on what they're pulling off.

But I believe there are no real limits to adventure. Each wave of athletes just takes it a step further, then another step further. After all, before Warren Harding and his gang of siege climbers got up the Nose in 1958, El Capitan itself was widely believed to be unclimbable. By now, fifty-seven years later, the Nose has been climbed free (Lynn Hill), free in a single day (Lynn again, as well as Tommy Caldwell), and in two hours, twenty-three minutes, and forty-six seconds (Hans Florine's and my speed record).

I'm sure there will come a time in the future when everything that I've done will be regarded as mundane. Someday climbers will consider 5.12 totally casual. They'll warm up on 5.14a. Ascents such as my free solos of Moonlight Buttress and Half Dome will be relegated to the history books, interesting for their time but no longer a big deal.

• • • •

A criticism you sometimes hear about climbing is that it's selfish. Putting up a new route, after all, does nothing to improve the human condition. Yet there's a kind of paradox, as I see it, in the fact that the public's enthusiasm for the kinds of climbing I've done since 2008 has led to sponsorship, commercials, and media coverage, which in turn have allowed me to pour money and motivation into trying to improve the lives of some of the least fortunate people on earth, those living marginalized lives in Africa or on Native American reservations in this country.

It was climbing, starting with our expedition to Chad in 2010, that awakened me to the plight of those impoverished peoples, and it was the money I made as a high-profile climber that allowed me to try to do something about it. Long before I started the Honnold Foundation, when people asked me which nonclimbers I most admired, I cited guys like Warren Buffett and Bill Gates. Billionaires who used their riches to address problems of environmental degradation and income inequality, and to provide educational opportunities to the disadvantaged. Today I'd add Elon Musk to the list—a business magnate and engineer who's reinventing the world.

With my Honnold Foundation, what I really hope to do in the coming years is to improve the lives of the most vulnerable people in the world in a way that helps the environment. To support projects that both help the earth and help lift people out of poverty.

I feel obligated to do something along those lines just because of the privileged life I've been given. But I'm doing it publicly in the hope that it will inspire more good deeds from others. Either way, I'd be donating some of my income, just so that I could sleep well at night. But by doing it publicly through the foundation, I'm hoping to inspire others to do the same—or at least to think about the issues more and reflect on their own lifestyles.

And in a more self-serving sense, it's good to have a hobby, particularly as I get older and pure rock climbing becomes less of a dominant force in my life. It's fun to work on a side project and learn new things.

Hand in hand with the critique that climbing is selfish is the claim that climbing is useless. But I think that perfecting your skills on rock (or ice and snow) ends up improving you in other ways. I fully believe that what I've learned from climbing translates into other aspects of life. Figuring out how to suppress my fear while free soloing, I'm pretty sure, has helped me suppress my fear of, say, public speaking. It's certainly helped cure my shyness, which, if you can believe my childhood pal Ben Smalley, was close to pathological. And if the kind of climbing I do inspires others to push their own limits, that's not a bad thing.

At the same time, I'd never set myself up as an "inspirational speaker." It's just not in my nature to turn my own experience into a soapbox from which to preach to others how they should live their lives. Some climbers have no trouble doing just that. For instance, Reinhold Messner, the first guy to climb the fourteen 8,000-meter peaks and the first guy to climb Everest solo without bottled oxygen, published a book in 1996 whose English title is Moving Mountains: Lessons on Life and Leadership. Each chapter ends with very didactic advice, under the headings "Application" and "Action." A sample: "Devise a wise risk management plan of action." Or, "Pursue a course of action that demands the exercise of your best qualities of character."

You can turn this whole inspirational thing on its head. Every once in a while, I hear that somebody thinks I'm a bad role model for kids. The argument goes something like this: Some kid sees a film like Alone on the Wall and decides he wants to try free solo-ing. Doesn't have the judgment yet to know how to stay safe. In the worst scenario, the kid gets on some route right at his limit, loses his cool, and falls off.

Well, I challenge those critics to cite a single case in which a climbing accident has been caused by some youngster trying to emulate me. It just doesn't work that way. If you've never free soloed before, you're likely to get twelve feet off the ground, freak out, and back off.

Climbers pushing the limits of their "sport" are pretty self-motivated. They're driven by the challenge itself, not by the urge to imitate some badass hero. For that matter, sailing across the Atlantic in 1492 was a pretty dangerous business. A scholar has calculated that on any voyage from Europe to the New World during the Renaissance, you stood a one-in-three chance of dying. But I doubt that anybody in Spain accused Columbus of being a bad role model for kids.

Anyway, I've never told anyone else (except maybe Tommy) that they ought to try free soloing or speed linkups involving simul-climbing or daisy soloing. I've even done the opposite, like throwing in that little disclaimer in a voice-over in Honnold 3.0. In effect, "Don't try this at home"—though that was also sort of a joke.

If what I do inspires others, that's fine. But that's not why I do it. No matter how much pressure sponsors or the media might put on me to try something rad (and by and large, they don't apply that kind of pressure), the ultimate decision is mine. I've walked away from more climbs than I can count, just because I sensed that things were not quite right. It's a deeply subjective decision, a combination of my mood and the vibe of the place and the weather. It's nothing I can precisely quantify, more like a vague feeling that some days are just not the right day.

. . . .

As the milestone of turning thirty fast approaches, I've had to think long and hard about my personal life. In the end, do I want to "settle down," move into an apartment and stop living in my van, get married, have kids, and inevitably scale down my ambition—and if so, when? How soon?

Whatever the statistics are about athletes being past their prime at thirty, in climbing there are stellar counterexamples. At thirty-seven, Tommy Caldwell is still cranking as hard as he ever did. Whether or not little Fitz convinces him to cut back on his risk-taking—and so far, there's little evidence of that—I remain in awe of his accomplishments, his determination, and his talent. Peter Croft is another climber I deeply admire. At fifty-seven, he's still climbing nearly as hard as he did in his late twenties, when he free soloed Astroman and the Rostrum in a single day. He has a circuit of 5.13 sport routes that he does in the Owens River Gorge every week. He's still shockingly fit. When I was an up-and-coming young climber, Peter seemed like a rock god—he was "the Man." Now I respect him not so much as a hero as for his whole climbing career. He's still passionate, but he only climbs what he cares about. I hope I can be like him when I get to that age.

In the fall of 2014, Stacey and I had another one of our periodic spats. The same old issues reared their heads—the questions of marriage, of kids down the line, of where and how to live. She really wanted to get on with her career as a nurse, not just follow me around from crag to crag or country to country. Our quarrel basically revolved around the idea of commitment. She wanted more commitment to the relationship on my part, while I still cherished the freedom to roam and see where things might take me.

So I sat down and made two separate plans for 2015. One was a program of traveling and climbing, tempered with Stacey time. The other was a program of pure climbing.

Stacey finally pulled the plug for good in December 2014, though we'd been talking about the issues for weeks and her decision came as no surprise. Having completed a graduate program in nursing the previous summer, she now moved to Salt Lake City and got a full-time job. And this time, when she said it was over, it felt final in a way it never had before.

Thank God it wasn't a bitter breakup. We didn't scream at each other. There was no major drama. We parted because in the long run what each of us wanted out of life was incompatible with the other's plans. We'll still be friends, eventually.

There was a lot of sadness on both sides. I felt the loss of something I might never find again. I had felt for years that I wanted to be with Stacey for a very long time, and she was the one woman I could imagine having kids with some day. I've never had a girlfriend I was half so serious about. I continue to admire and respect her as a person.

At the same time, I felt an unexpected surge of liberation. Ahead of me stretched another full year of great adventures and new climbs. Patagonia, Australia, maybe Pakistan. . . . I used to say that I couldn't think six months ahead, let alone five years. For the first time ever, I can now see five years into the future. I've got at least five years of climbing and exploring at my highest level ahead of me. Maybe more.

A shrink might accuse me of clinging to my boyhood, of refusing to grow up. But boyhood, in the best sense, is all tied up with adventure. Climbing as well as you can for as long as you can is a boyhood dream, even if you're about to turn thirty.

What matters most to me right now is that climbing is still totally involving. I'm still learning new tricks of the trade, from direct aid to mixed rock and ice in the great ranges. I'm still exploring my limits. I may talk about what it would mean to free solo El Cap, but I also have a whole notebook in my head of potential projects on my tick list. I generally don't like to share these publicly—not because I'm being coy, or because I'm afraid somebody else might poach them, but simply because I don't like to create expectations. I don't want to feel obligated to climb in any way, and I worry that creating expectations ahead of time would add external pressure.

What keeps me motivated is an insatiable hunger and curiosity. The best way I can sum it up is to paraphrase the ending of my op-ed piece for the New York Times.

The mountains are calling, and I must go.

Author's Note

On May 16, 2015, as this book was headed to press, Dean Potter and his partner, Graham Hunt, died in a BASE jumping accident in Yosemite.

Though we were never close friends, news of Dean's death shook me in a profound way. Especially when I was younger, Dean had a powerful influence on my own climbing, and I looked up to him as a role model. I'd always thought that he would live to an old age because, despite how his deeds may have looked to others, he was actually fairly conservative. But accidents happen, especially in BASE jumping, and although I was shocked I couldn't say I was completely surprised.

The most striking thing about Dean was his uncompromising approach to his arts: climbing, BASE jumping, and highlining. He devoted himself to the perfection of his craft, pursuing each aspect with limitless passion. Never one to follow the herd, Dean was always out in front, forging a new path. His vision took the sport of climbing in entirely new directions, from speed soloing in the 1990s to freeBASE a decade later. He was the true nonconformist, devoted to his art but unconcerned about legality or other people's opinions.

Dean Potter will live on through all of us whom he inspired.

Acknowledgments

From Alex Honnold

My biggest thanks must go to David Roberts, without whom this book would not exist. He did all the heavy lifting in trying to shape my climbing trips into a readable form. I wouldn't have trusted anyone else with the job, and I appreciate how much he helped me throughout the whole process.

My sister, Stasia Honnold, also helped me immensely with the editing process. I'm very lucky to have a sister who knows me so well and is always willing to help. And, most important, she's always inspiring me to try to live a better life.

The climbing and travel in this book wouldn't have been possible without the support of my entire extended family. I'm grateful that everyone has always encouraged my adventures and not questioned my decision to take a different path.

Thanks also to my sponsors—The North Face, Goal Zero, Black Diamond, La Sportiva, and Maxim Ropes—for providing me with the opportunities to push my climbing all over the world. Without sponsorship, I would just be a dirtbag climber living in a van. Oh, wait. . . .

The guys at Sender Films and Big UP Productions deserve thanks for so well documenting my climbing. Without their storytelling, I would not be on the same path.

And, of course, thanks to all my climbing partners over the years. I feel uncomfortable singling anyone out, since I've climbed with so many people over the years and learned something different from each of them. But a few partners have been formative to my climbing:

- Josh McCoy, for teaching me how to trad climb, and for still adventuring with me whenever possible.
- Chris Weidner, for many great climbing trips and for always providing a home base for me.
- Cedar Wright and Tommy Caldwell, for participating in some of the biggest climbs of my life and for always being good friends.

And finally, thanks to the general climbing community, which makes this entire life possible. I'm grateful to be part of such a big and inclusive family.

From David Roberts

I'd like to acknowledge a number of people who contributed vitally to *Alone on the Wall*. Our editor at W. W. Norton & Company, Starling Lawrence, not only saw the potential appeal of the book at once, but skillfully guided it through the many bumps from proposal to finished text with his usual deft erudition and wry commentary. This is Alex's first but my third book with Star, and I couldn't be happier in our teamwork or more confident of his wisdom as editor. Star's assistant, Ryan Harrington, got deeply involved in the gestation of our book, and went out of his way to fix more potential snags than most books run into. Thanks, Ryan, for your calm and canny work. Our copy editor, Kathleen Brandes, performed a careful and intelligent job of catching the typos, redundancies, contradictions, and omissions in our text.

We're grateful to the several photographers whose excellent images grace the two photo inserts in this book, capturing Alex's genius in a way that words are often incapable of. They include Jimmy Chin, Ben Moon, Andrew Burr, Peter Mortimer and Nick Rosen at Sender Films, Renan Ozturk, Tommy Caldwell, Cedar Wright, Rolando Garibotti, and Alex's mother, Dierdre Wolownick.

The parts of the book written in my voice depended crucially on the commentary of others. For their insights into what makes Alex tick, I thus salute Chris Weidner, Tommy Caldwell, Cedar Wright, Renan Ozturk, Alex Lowther, Peter Mortimer, Mark Synnott, Jimmy Chin, Freddie Wilkinson, and Stacey Pearson.

Our literary agent, Stuart Krichevsky, contributed an extraordinary range of judgments, negotiations, and even interventions to make this book better than it otherwise might have been. In a professional life as busy as Stuart's, it's almost a luxury to lavish such care and affection on a single project. This is my fourteenth book with Stuart, and it not only never gets old—I often pinch myself in gratitude to have such a stalwart and *engagé* manager and pinch hitter in my lineup. The same goes for Stuart's tireless and always accessible colleagues, Shana Cohen and Ross Harris.

Several friends who read the book in manuscript offered valuable suggestions. For that, I heartily thank Bill Briggs, Ed Ward, Molly Birnbaum, and Matt Hale (who also helped me immensely with the photo selection and procurement).

Finally, I owe my deepest debt and gratitude to Alex Honnold himself. When I first hung out with him at Smith Rock in 2010, as I researched a profile for *Outside* magazine, I was at once taken aback by Alex's brashness and obsessive focus and charmed by his wit, intelligence, and compassion. It's not always a good thing for a feature writer unstintingly to admire his subject's achievements— the writer's job, after all, is partly to poke holes in the subject's persona—but I was blown away by Alex's climbing.

From that initial week together, a friendship grew. It felt awkward at times, given the age gap between us, and given the fact that my own best climbing lay decades in the rearview mirror while Alex's gleamed through the windshield ahead of him. But we worked out a kind of teasing camaraderie that would fuel our collaboration.

Alex is a good writer—good enough, as I told him in the early spring of 2014, that he could have written this book by himself. But writing, he confessed, was slow and painful for him—and besides, it threatened to take time away from climbing. I was deeply flattered when he agreed to work on *Alone on the Wall* together. Whatever the virtues of our book, they spring directly from Alex's character— not only as a climber but also as a human being.

Index